DO MORE ART PRINT

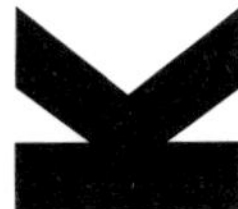

First published in Great Britain in 2025 by Laurence King, an imprint of The Orion Publishing Group Ltd, Carmelite House, 50 Victoria Embankment, London EC4Y 0DZ

An Hachette UK Company

The authorised representative in the EEA is Hachette Ireland, 8 Castlecourt Centre, Dublin 15, D15 XTP3, Ireland (email: info@hbgi.ie)

10 9 8 7 6 5 4 3 2 1

A CIP catalogue record for this book is available from the British Library.

ISBN (Hardback) 978 1 39962 659 0
ISBN (eBook) 978 1 39962 661 3

Commissioning Editor: Laura Paton
Project Editor: Sarah Fortune
Art Director: Liam Relph
Designer: Hannah Beatrice Owens
Picture Researcher: Susannah Jayes
Senior Production Controller: Sarah Cook
Origination by F1 Colour
Printed in Dubai by Oriental Press

Back cover: Eve Blackwood, *Rainbow Stag Beetle*, 2024

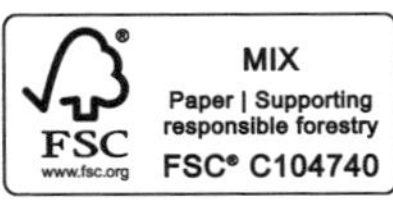

www.laurenceking.com
www.orionbooks.co.uk

DO MORE ART PRINT

Eve Blackwood

Laurence King

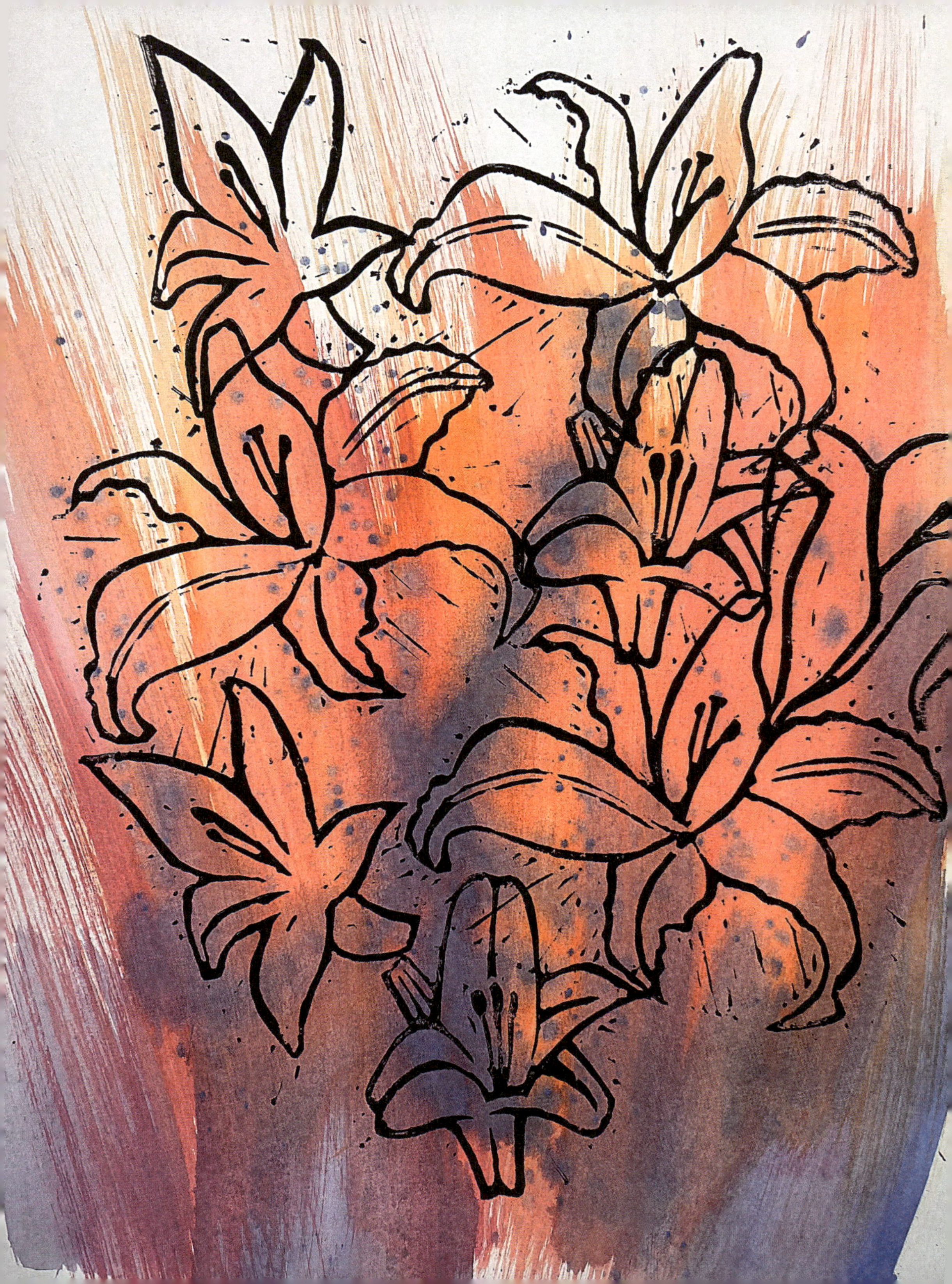

CONTENTS

Eve Blackwood, *Lilies*, lino print, paint on paper, 2024

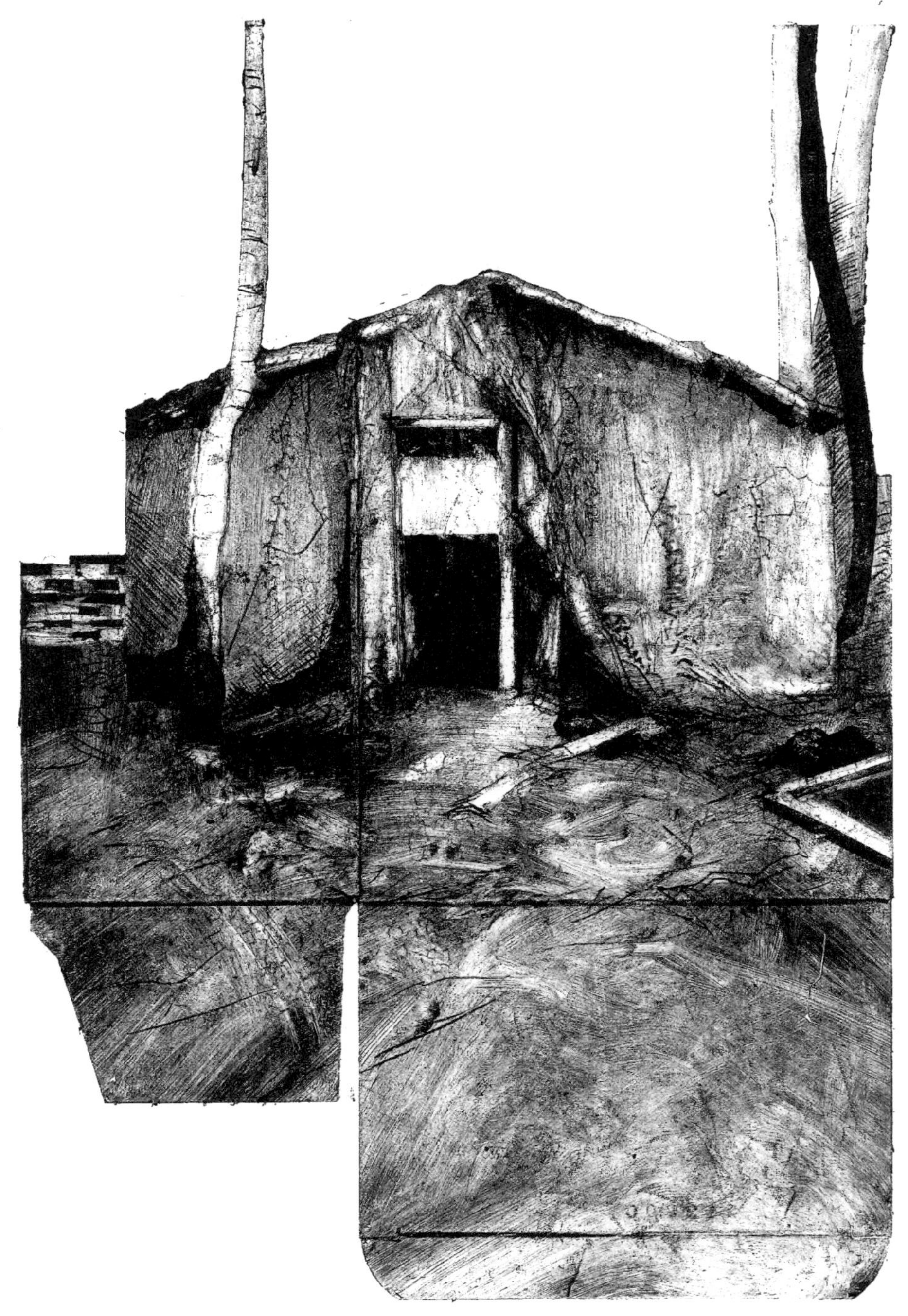

Karen Wicks, *RAF Tilstock Hut 1*, collagraph, ink on card, 2020

GO FORTH AND MULTIPLY

So, what's the big deal with printmaking? Why should you be interested in it? Well, it's an incredibly varied and fascinating way to make images that can be reproduced and distributed, so you can share your art and ideas far and wide, or just enjoy the process for yourself.

Printmaking is accessible to people of all ages, abilities and levels of creative confidence. In this book, we will look at printing techniques that don't even require a press, others that do and artists who are experimenting with printing in an exciting and inspiring way.

This book will show you how to make incredibly sophisticated prints from the simplest equipment. Here is an example of a beautifully haunting image made from a box. One of the things that I absolutely love about this print is that the plate adds to the character and shape. Karen Wicks is careful to preserve the nature of the flattened box by incorporating the embossed best-before date, the flaps and the folds into her composition. The throwaway nature of the printing plate matches the subject of abandoned places from which she draws inspiration. This is a great example of how an incredibly evocative and atmospheric image can be created from a piece of recycling.

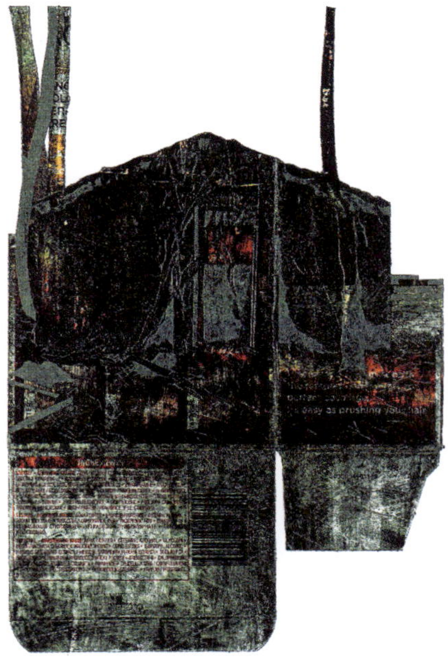

A flattened box is used for a printing plate. It has had a coat of shellac varnish applied to it to make it more robust.

JUMP ONBOARD THIS HISTORICAL JUGGERNAUT

So, how can you be part of the story of print? Well, printmaking is simply the act of transferring an image or design onto a surface like paper or cloth, using ink or paint. This is usually done using specially prepared plates, blocks or stencils.

There are three main categories in printmaking: planographic, relief and intaglio. Each has its own distinctive style and qualities, imposed by the tools, materials and printing methods. Some involve printing from a flat surface (planographic), some from raised surfaces (relief) and intaglio uses engraved surfaces. The image opposite is an example of an etching which is part of the intaglio school of printing.

One of the main advantages of printmaking, and a major reason it became so popular, is the ability to create multiple copies of each print. Amanda Outcalt really exploits this by embellishing her prints individually to create unique works of art. Her etchings of animals are made on copper printing plates that have been cut into the shape of the animal, which means she can change the composition of each print depending on where she places the image on the paper. The print is further modified because she hand colours with pencil and paint and, in this case, adds an embroidered crown. The crown creates a feeling that her *Queen of the Sea* is all dressed up with nowhere to go. This morose manatee's skin has a complex surface quality built up through a combination of marks and tone which show the possibilities of etching, a long-established form of printmaking.

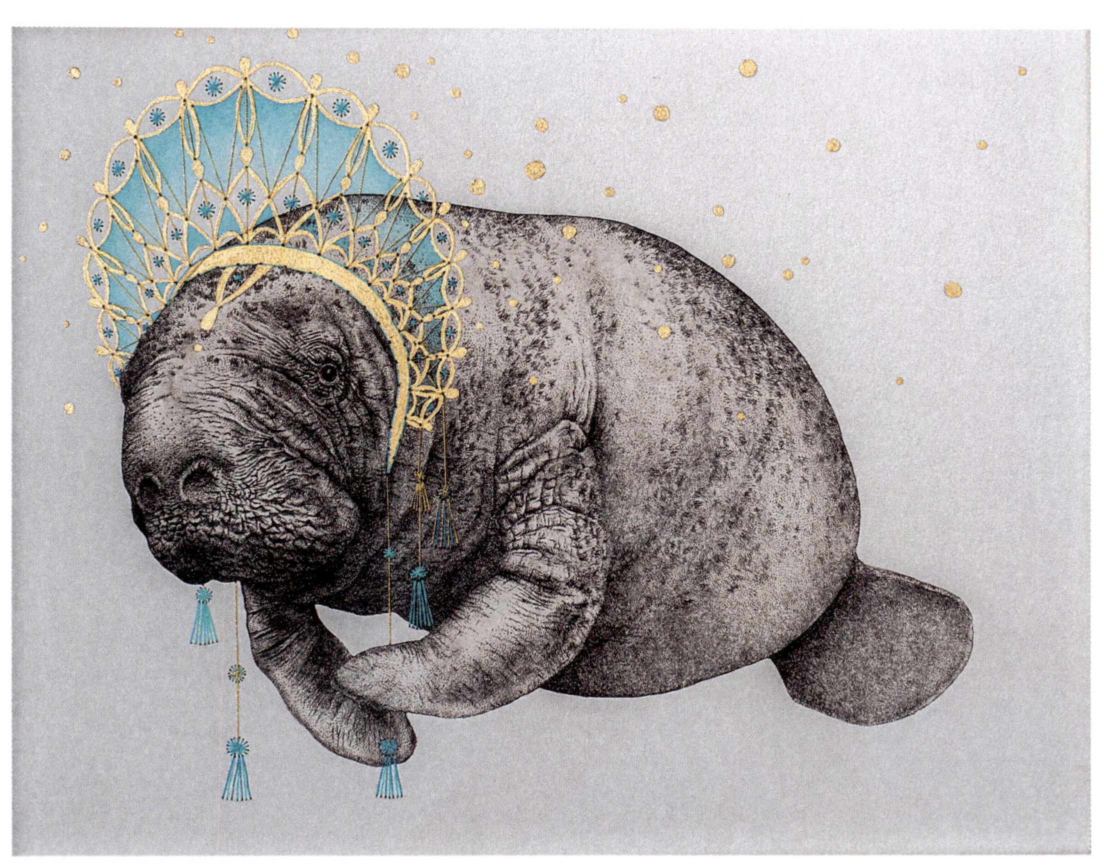

Amanda Outcalt, *Queen of the Sea*, intaglio, gold leaf, acrylic ink and stitched thread on paper, 2023

KIT AND CABOODLE

Basic equipment

Handy basic equipment that you might already own includes: a flat glass plate such as a chopping board, or an unmarked non-stick baking tray; a sheet of plastic or acetate; scissors; glue; paper and card; a craft knife; a pair of compasses or a bradawl.

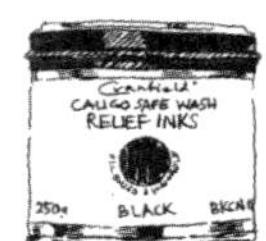

Printing inks

There is a variety of different printing inks: water-based (best for domestic use as no solvents are needed to clean up); oil-based; fabric ink; and screen-print ink. Some inks are sticky and others silky. Monoprinting requires a silky intaglio ink that can move freely on the printing plate. This is also true for collagraphs, drypoint and etching. Relief printing, like lino, needs a sticky block-print ink that will stick to the printing blocks. Acrylic paint can be used for printing, with or without an added printing medium. Ink pads are good for smaller stamps. Specialist inks for printing on fabric are also available.

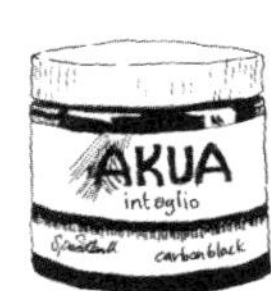

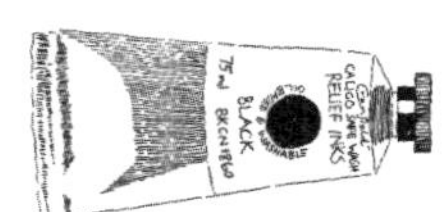

Colours

Every colour can be mixed from red, yellow, blue, black and white. Practise adding small amounts of colours to achieve the hues you want. Mix this on your inking plate using an offcut of a hard card.

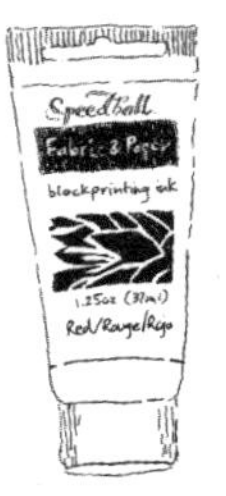

Roller/brayer

This is a hard rubber roller used for applying the ink to the surface of your printing plate.

Inking plate

Inks are laid out and mixed on a flat, wipeable surface before transferring the ink to the brayer. For this, you could use a sheet of acetate or glass, a plastic paint palette or a new non-stick baking sheet. You can also use this surface to make monoprints.

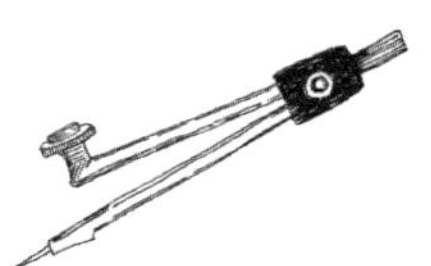

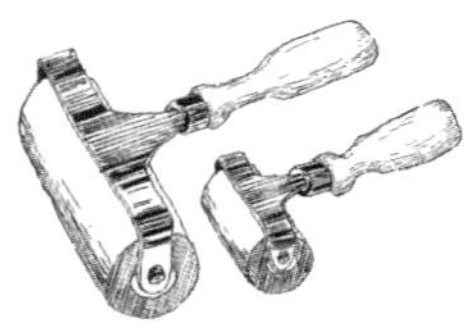

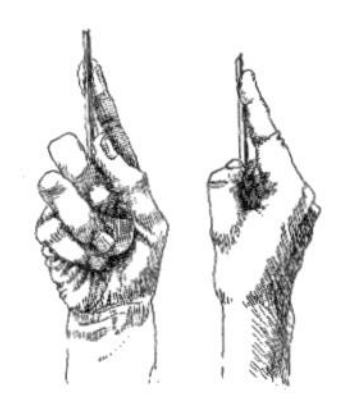

Linocutting tools

A good basic set of these tools will allow you to make a variety of marks and help you to get to grips with relief printing.

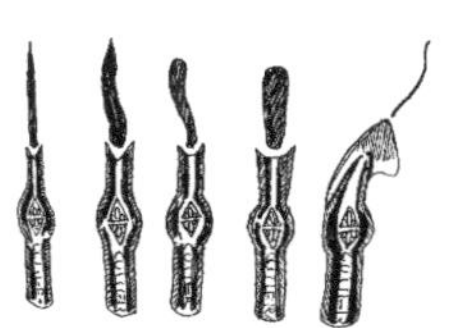

Cutting blades come in three shapes and a variety of sizes. V-shaped blades are good for fine lines, U-shaped blades are good for gouging out large areas and knife-edged blades are good for defining edges or creating very fine lines.

The handles of linocutting tools are shaped to nestle into the shape of your hand, so you hold them against the heel of your hand to exert pressure. Your index finger should be used to guide the blade.

Baren

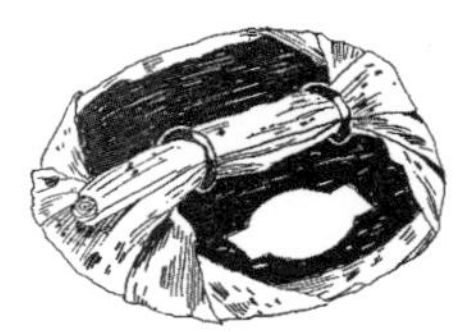

To take an impression from a printing plate you need to apply pressure. You can do this with or without a printing press. A baren is a disc-like hand tool which is used in a circular rubbing motion to apply pressure to the back of the printing paper. This transfers the image from the printing plate. You could substitute this with a clean roller, a wooden spoon or the side of your hand. For Gelli prints, a pile of heavy art books left over time allows the image to stick to the paper.

Printing press

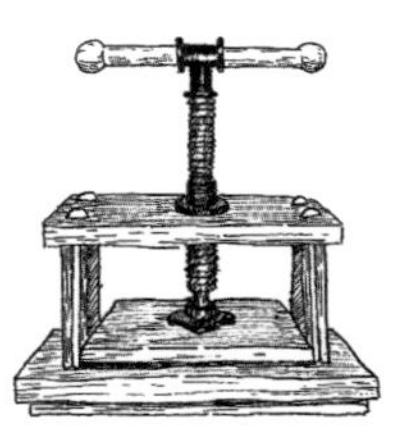

Printing presses come in many different types, sizes and shapes to suit your budget and the amount of space you have. Some are wooden and come in kit form to be made at home. Metal ones are heavy but will exert more pressure, which is good for intaglio printing and embossing. You can also turn an existing piece of equipment like a flower press, pasta maker or die-cut press into a printing press. Joining a printmaking workshop is a good way to access a range of presses and other specialist printing equipment.

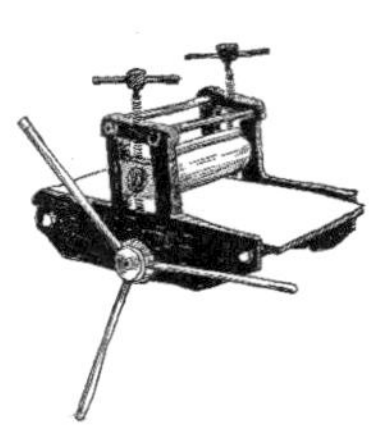

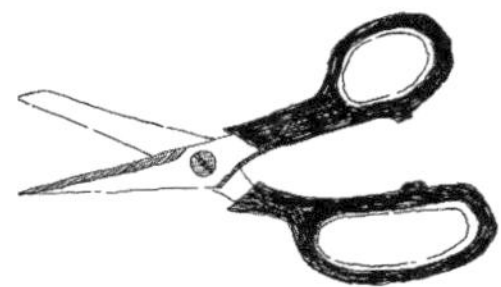

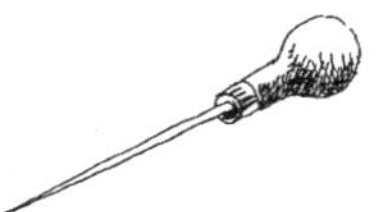

SURFACES

You can print on a range of surfaces. The main one we think of is paper, so let's start there.

PAPER

Weight

Paper weight is often measured in grams per square metre (gsm). It comes in different weights: from 80gsm (photocopy paper), which is great for test prints, to 330gsm and up (almost as thick as card), which is good for hand-printed stationery. A thicker paper will be more robust, allowing you to dampen it, which softens and opens up its fibrous weave. It will emboss, creating a raised design on the paper as you run it through a printing press. This is a great choice for drypoints, etching and collagraphs, and relief printing if you want an embossed effect.

Tooth

This describes the surface texture of the paper. More tooth means it will be rougher, which can help ink cling to the surface. This texture will show through your print. You do want some texture: if your paper is too glossy or metallic, it may not let your print set, leading to smearing or, at worst, your print not drying.

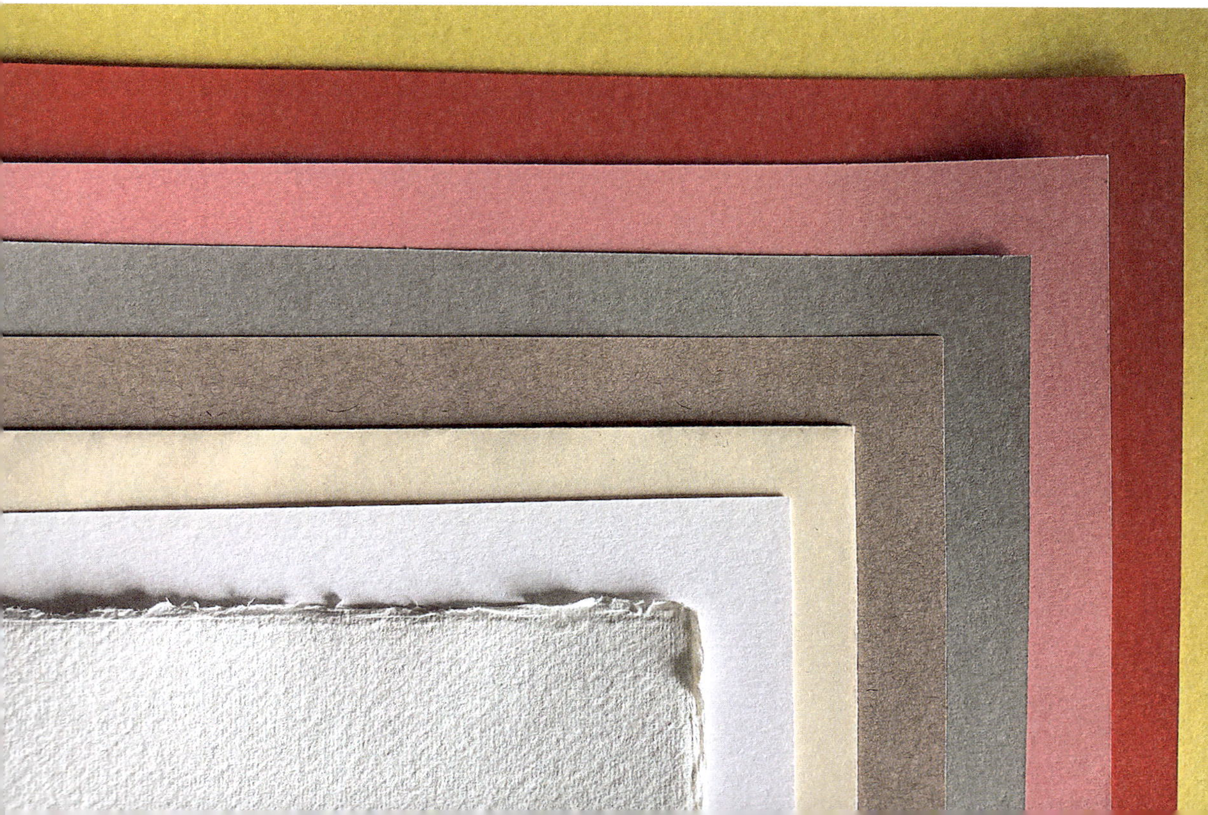

TYPES OF PAPER

Cartridge paper

A medium weight (140gsm), smooth, white cartridge paper is a good choice for creating prints with good definition.

Coloured paper

When producing a multicolour print, you will use the colour of the paper as one of your colours. If you choose to print onto a coloured paper, test this first because some vibrant colours may affect the colour of the subsequent printed ink layers.

Watercolour paper

A heavier, wood pulp-based paper, printed on when damp, is good for achieving an embossed print. Hot-press watercolour paper is usually smoother than cold press.

Cotton rag

Also known as rag paper, or 'rag', this is made using cotton fibres or cotton from used cloth (rags) as the primary material. Most specialist printing paper will have some cotton content. Cotton paper is stronger and more durable than wood pulp-based paper and absorbs ink more effectively. It's good for embossing.

Archival paper

This is acid-free paper that will not yellow with age. It's good for prints you want to keep for a long time.

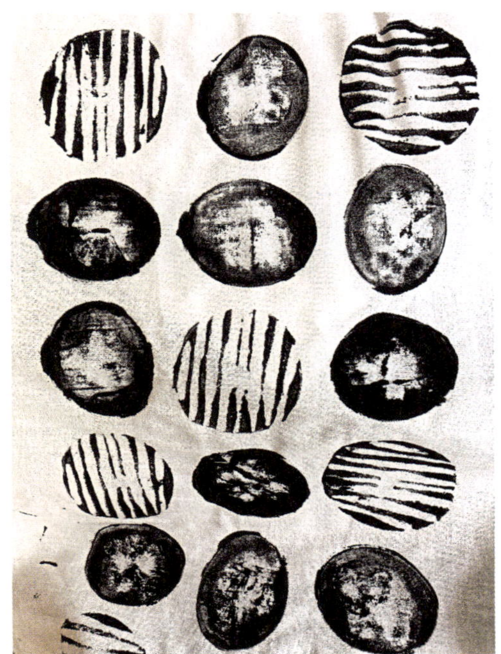

FABRIC

Specialist inks make permanent prints on fabric. However, as these inks require ironing to set them, some synthetic fabrics may not be a good choice. Fine-weave cotton will give well-defined prints, whereas a more utilitarian look can be achieved using linen or canvas. Always wash, dry and iron fabric before printing.

OTHER SURFACES

Other surfaces include wood and clay. Your uninked lino plate can be pressed into clay to emboss it before it is fired. Wood should be sanded before printing and sealed after.

THE POSSIBILITIES OF PRINT

FINGERPRINTING

Anything with an irregular surface can be inked up and used to make a print. One of the first tools we come across as young artists are our fingers. Artist and designer Saul Steinberg took the creative possibilities of this and ran with it, creating a series of inspired fingerprint images. This one is particularly clever because it deals with issues of identity and individualism. The unique nature of the fingerprint is in direct contrast with the salaryman shirt and tie of the anonymous worker featured. The brilliance of Saul Steinberg's fingerprint art lies in the playful way that he interprets the possibilities of this most accessible of printmaking techniques. Here, he uses a stencil to limit the print, which allows him to create the tie and jacket lapels. By leaving the face featureless, he creates anonymity with the very thing that makes us all individual - brilliant!

TRY IT YOURSELF

By limiting yourself to a very simple printing technique you have to draw on your creativity and sense of humour to make it engaging. How are you going to do that?

1. Using an ink pad to stain your fingertip, start by making prints on the paper, asking yourself: what can this misshapen printed lump be?

2. Introducing a small, equally simple, drawn character to interact with your fingerprint means you now have a story.

3. Maybe the fingerprint is a rock for someone to trip over? Or it's a boulder that someone is struggling to push or carry? Or now it's a balloon that has escaped from a distraught toddler?

The sky's the limit for your imagination and your fingerprint is the little red balloon floating in it.

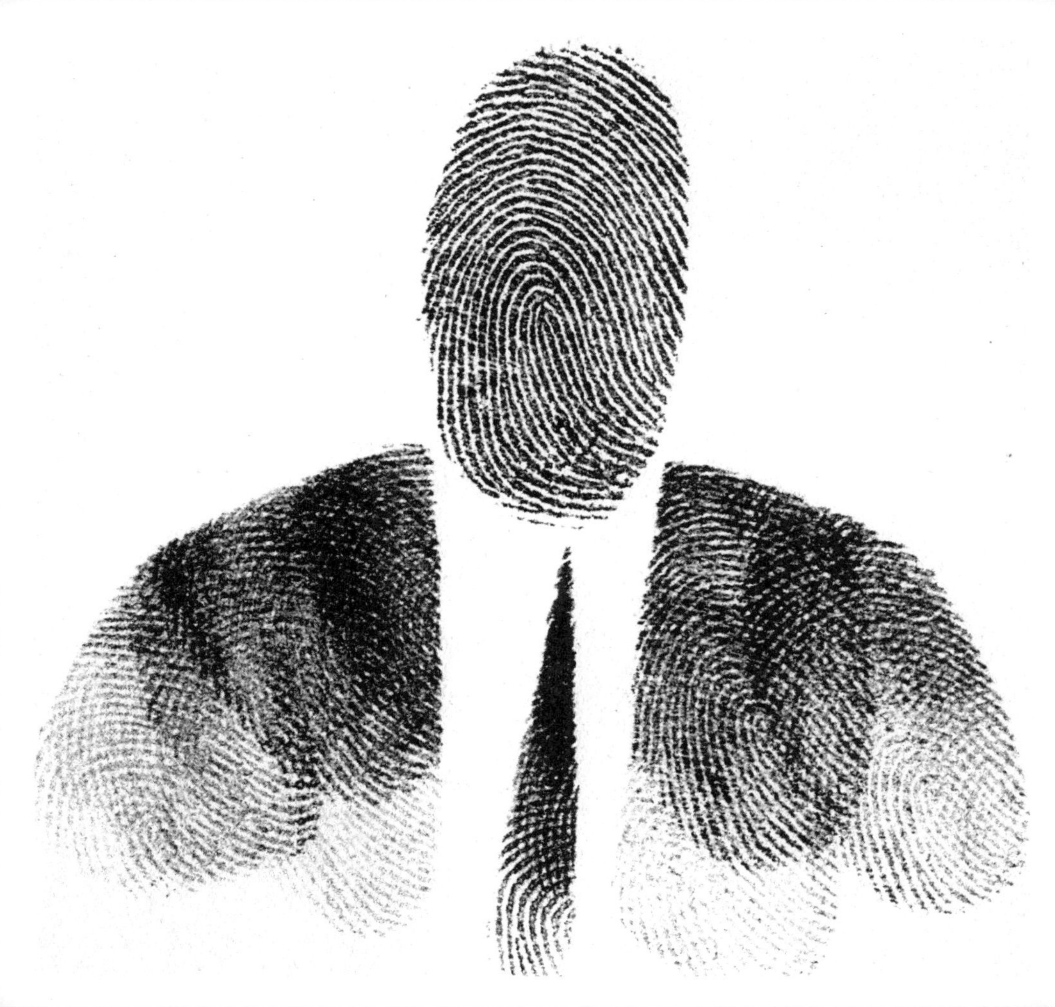

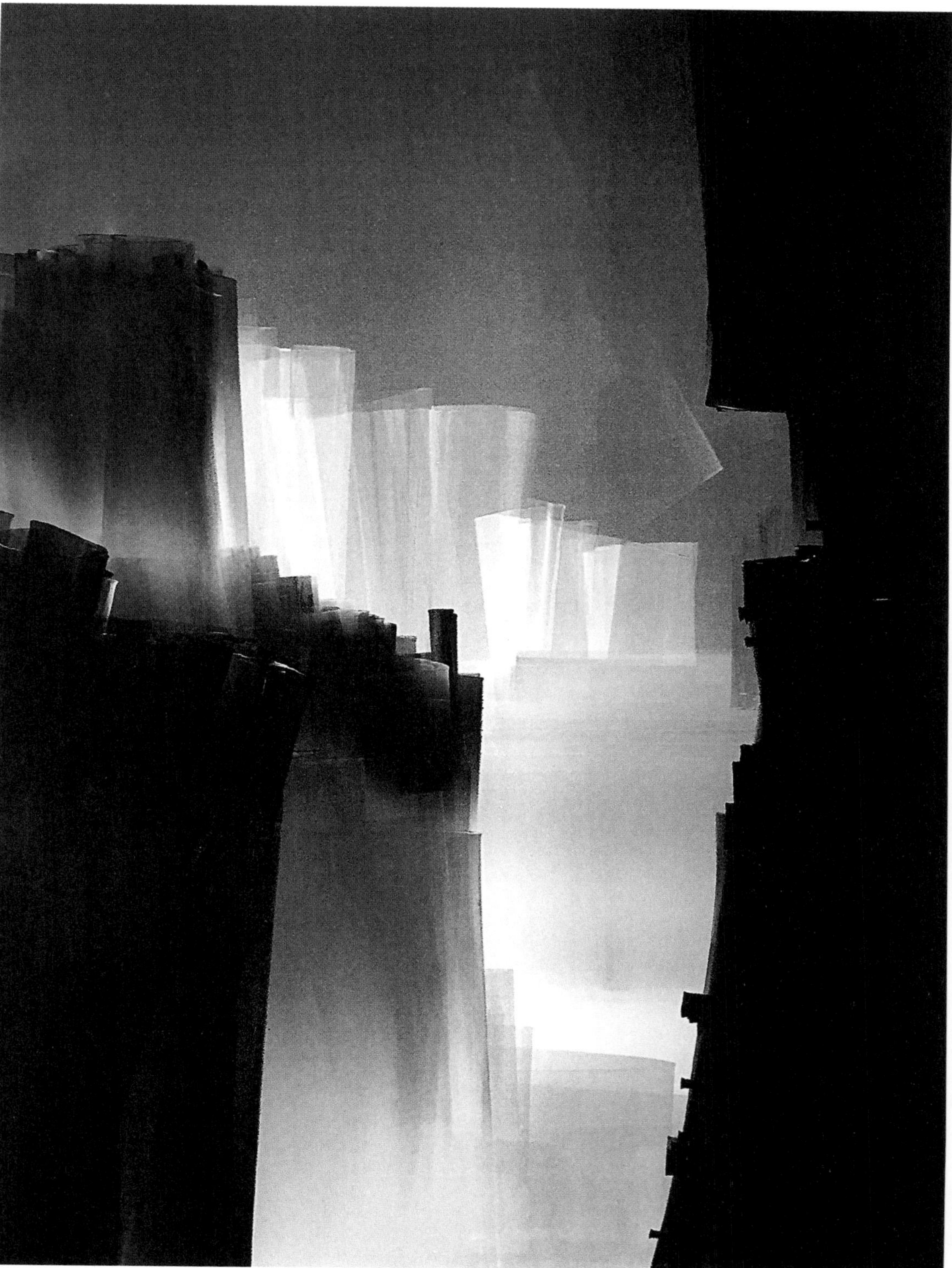

THERE IS POTENTIAL EVERYWHERE

Artist Koichi Yamamoto is a champion at seeing the potential in a misshapen inky splodge. He started to see the possibilities in the accidental prints that he made while cleaning his large printing rollers on lightweight waste paper. He took these as a starting point for a series of prints, appropriately, about human waste. Isn't it satisfying when the technique suits the subject matter? Koichi's method is a great eco-friendly way to clean your brayer because, by rolling the brayer on paper to remove the ink from it, you're limiting the amount of hot water and detergent that might otherwise be used to clean it.

Koichi Yamamoto started to notice that, as he did this, he was making large, monolithic cliffs of ink which he then built on to create foggy mountainscapes. These remind me of Ansel Adams' epic black-and-white photographs of Yosemite. Imposing and magnificent, these landscapes loom out of the fog, creating apocalyptic scenes. The enormous cliff face in the foreground is set off against the impression of a metropolis emerging in the smoggy distance. These prints are atmospheric and evocative, and even better for being a waste product. There really is potential everywhere.

Opposite: Koichi Yamamoto, *Todoroki*, monotype, ink on paper, 2019

FIND THE EXTRAORDINARY IN THE ORDINARY

Bryan Christopher Baker is an artist who saw the printmaking potential of an everyday object we are all familiar with: a common six-sided dice. When laying the dice out in a grid to form a large printable area, he is faced with a series of decisions: to allow the randomness of a throw to dictate the patterns, or to carefully place the dice to create a regular, predictable, but fascinatingly complex, lattice of dots. By making a print of them, the familiar dots on each face of the dice become something else: a pattern with a pleasing rhythm that dissociates them from their original purpose and transforms them into something new. Once Bryan has decided on his layout, he can place them on the bed of the printing press and ink them up. The resulting prints are varied in size, colour and pattern, but all have a pleasing mathematical logic.

When you start opening your eyes to everyday flat-surfaced objects with indents, or interesting patterns and textures, the printmaking possibilities of domestic items will start firing in your brain.
Look around you. What can you see that might have this exciting potential? Do you have a box full of discarded buttons, a cotton bobbin, interestingly shaped biscuit cutters, bubble wrap or a collection of plastic lids waiting to be recycled? All these things and more may have printing potential, and if you repeat them in the random or ordered way Bryan Christopher Baker does, you can create pleasing patterns of what we call repeating motifs. By planning your layout and colour palette, you can produce elegant and sophisticated prints from simple commonplace objects.

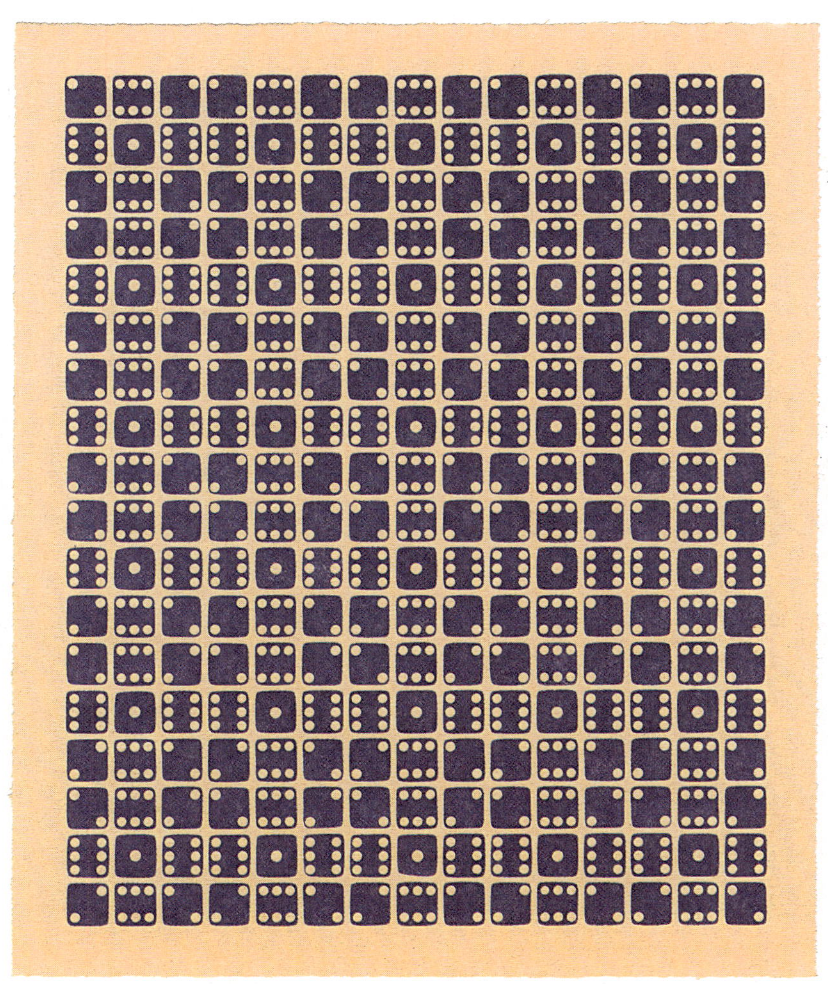

Bryan Christopher Baker, *Phoebe*, relief print, oil-based ink on paper, 2019

CREATE PATTERNS WITH HOUSEHOLD OBJECTS

Claire Drury has opened her eyes to the printing potential in her home to create this inventive and colourful print from household objects. Inspired by Eduardo Paolozzi's textile designs, she uses repetition to create groupings, patterns and rhythm in her design. Starting on a painted sheet of paper, she introduces areas of analogous greens and blues and other areas of complementary orange and orangey-red. The overall effect is fun and frenetic, full of visual interest and playful colour combinations.

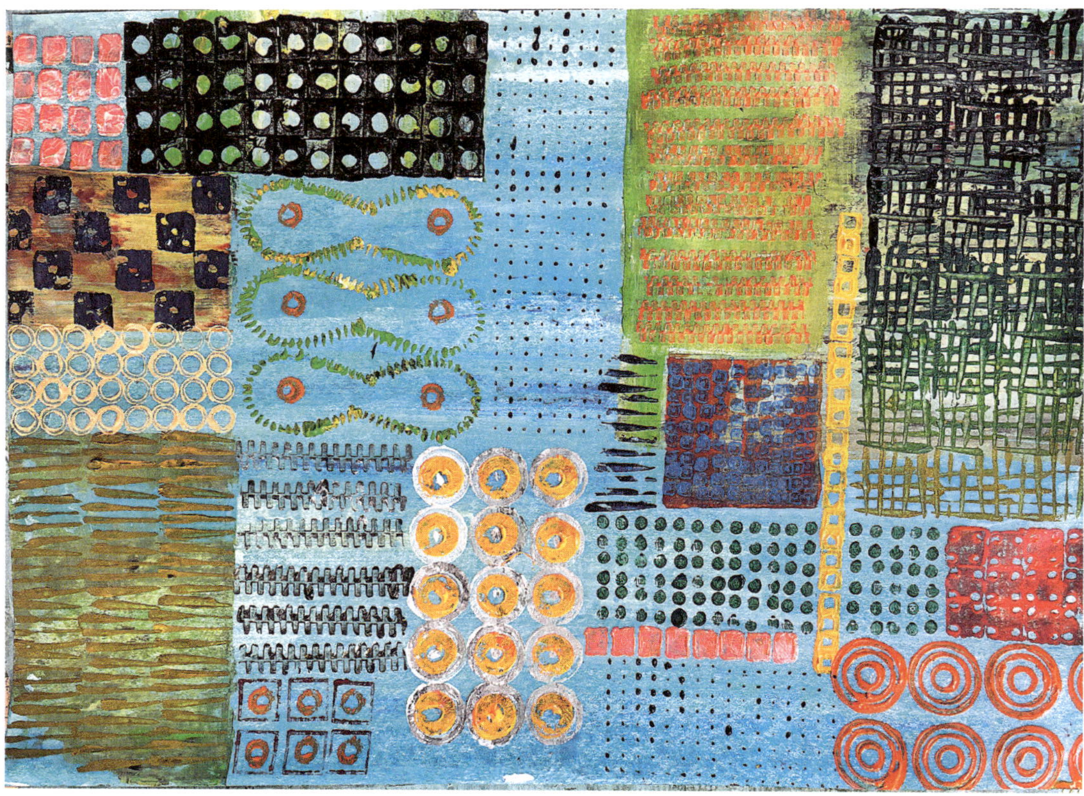

Claire Drury, *Summer Holidays*, found objects, acrylic and painted papers, 2024

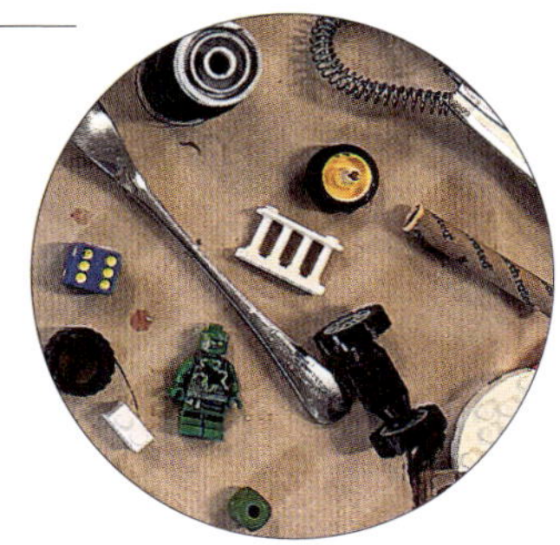

Identifying the potential

We can make prints from everyday objects by applying the basic principles of relief and planograph printmaking. When we think of planographic printing, we know that any flat surface that will take ink - a wine cork, for example - will allow us to make a print in the shape of that surface. From our understanding of relief printing, we know that anything that has a smooth surface with indentations, like a domino, will produce a patterned print.

Revealing hidden qualities

By slicing open a vegetable, you can create a flat surface to transfer ink, or reveal a hidden inner relief pattern that you can use to print.

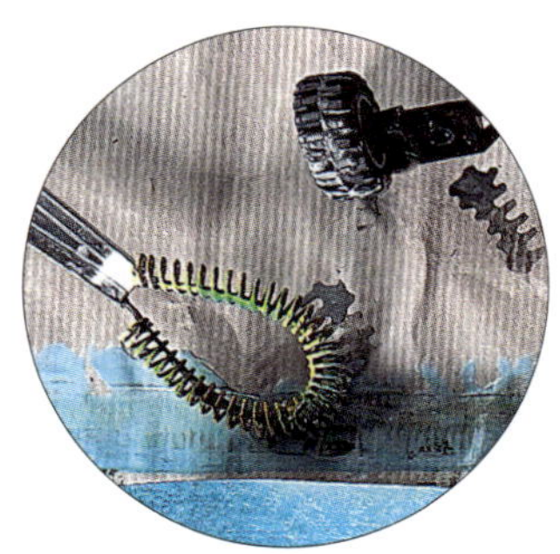

Inking up

Apply acrylic paint with a brush to achieve the added texture of brushstrokes. The paint can dry quickly, so you need to work fast and wash up as you go to avoid permanently painted objects or stiff paint brushes.

Creating a pattern

Rhythm is important to consider when creating a repeat print: what is the logic to your repeat and will you disrupt that predictability?

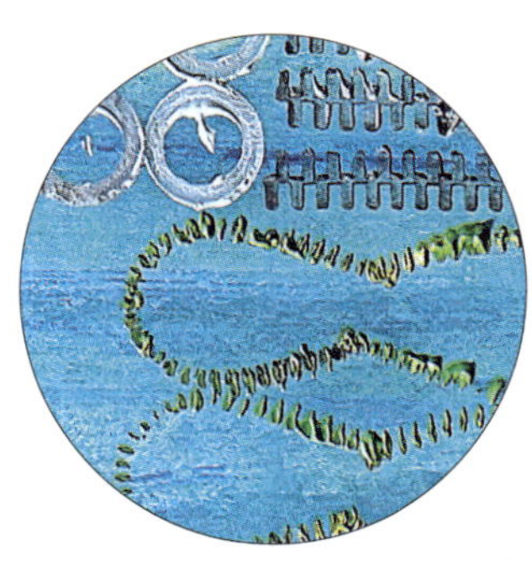

Colour combinations

Planning your colour palette can elevate your print. For example, a well-considered group of analogous colours can bring a sophisticated elegance.

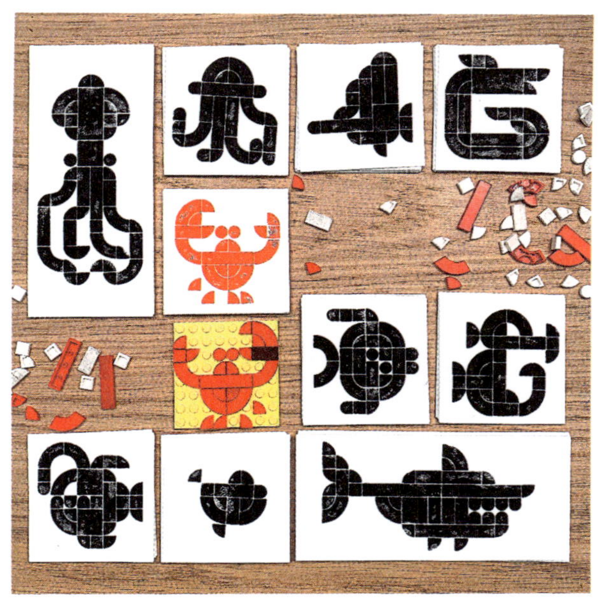

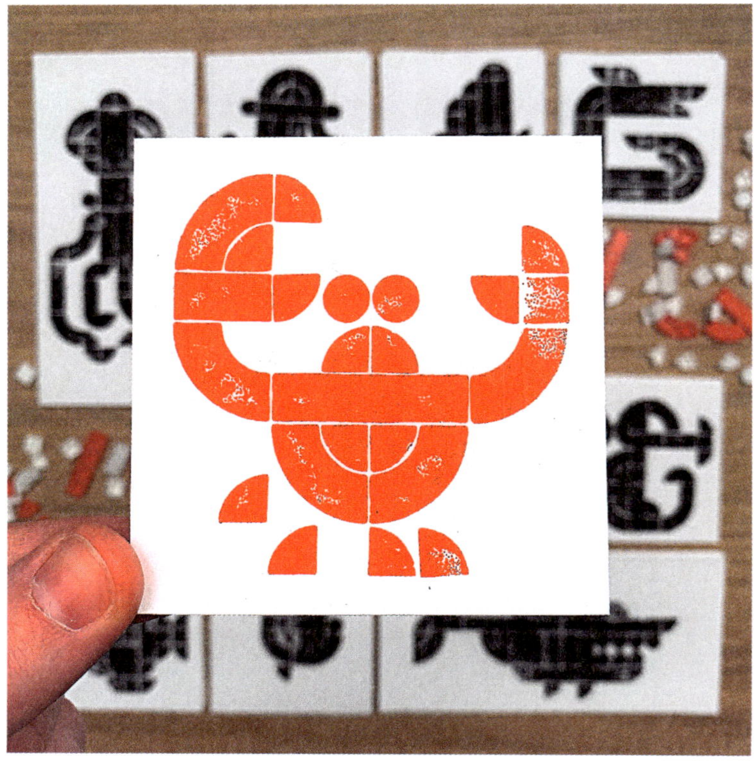

Kasey Golden, *Aquatic LEGO Prints*, relief ink on watercolour paper, 2023

MODULAR PRINTING

This is a fun way of repurposing that big box of toy bricks that has not been played with for years. Using one of those knobbly baseboards to secure your new printing blocks, you can start making recognisable shapes which, due to a construction set's modular nature, will look a bit pixelated.

Kasey Golden has used a variety of small, shiny, flat blocks from her construction set to create these simplified designs inspired by sea creatures. She has produced a series of appealing little emojis that capture the essence of these creatures in a fun way which echoes the playful nature of the original toy. Building up blocks of colour by placing the bricks adjacent to each other, she also occasionally leaves gaps to create eyes and the details around the shark's teeth. She adds movement in the free arrangement of the octopus' limbs and in the jaunty placement of the crab's feet and claws.

TRY IT YOURSELF

1. When you are working with such a limited system, you have to refine and reduce your design, being careful to preserve the character and proportions. The use of one colour helps to add to the bold graphic quality of these prints.

2. You could plan out your design beforehand or just get stuck in and try it out. There is a benefit to experimenting and seeing what the potential is. As you start to play, you may find a design emerges from this process.

3. Use the baseboard to arrange your bricks, pressing them firmly down. When you initially ink up the surface of the blocks with your roller, you might find they repel the ink. Repeated printing and inking will help make the ink stick more successfully and your succeeding prints will be darker.

4. Once you have inked up your printing-block arrangement, wipe the excess ink from the baseboard to preserve the clean look of the print.

TAKE INSPIRATION FROM YOUR SURROUNDINGS

Berlin-based collective Raubdruckerin, which roughly translates to 'pirate printer', has taken a guerilla approach to printmaking. Its members have made several editions of prints that record the often-overlooked diversity in the urban design that we trudge over every day. By inking up manhole covers, grates and street tiles, they have decorated T-shirts and bags which are emblazoned with these designs.

To do this successfully, they use a printing ink that can be washed away from the printing surface, but is still able to be fixed onto the fabric so the T-shirt or bag can be washed and retain the print. A card frame is also used to limit the area of the manhole cover that is printed, creating a nice crisp edge that adds to the graphic quality of the printed image. This is one of those lovely projects that opens our eyes to the world around us, encouraging us to notice details in our environment that are far too easy to miss.

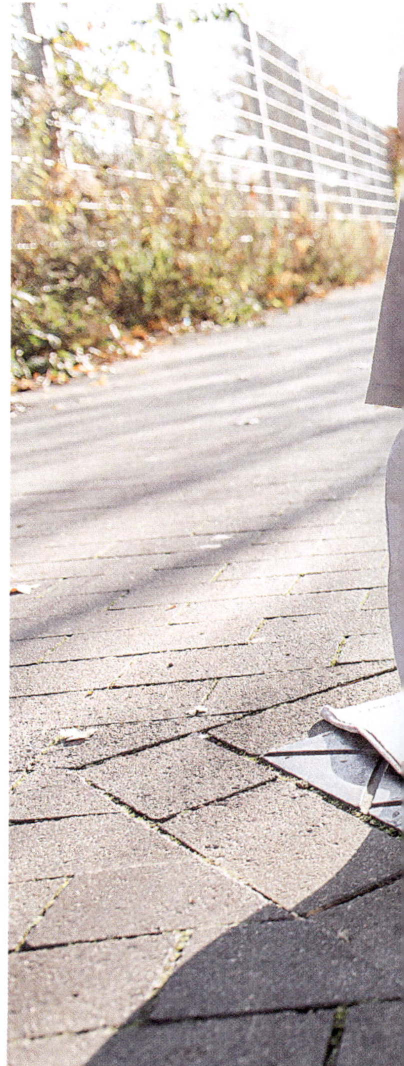

TRY IT YOURSELF

Swap paper for fabric
Decorating fabric is one of the earliest uses of printmaking and is still used today around the world on an industrial scale. Almost any printmaking technique that will work on paper will work on fabric.

Check your inks
It is vital that you use fabric-printing inks that are designed not to wash away when you wash your printed fabric. Fabric inks for block and screen printing are widely available and come in a range of colours. They usually have to be ironed to fix them.

Raubdruckerin,
Street Printing: Manhole Cover,
transfer print,
2017

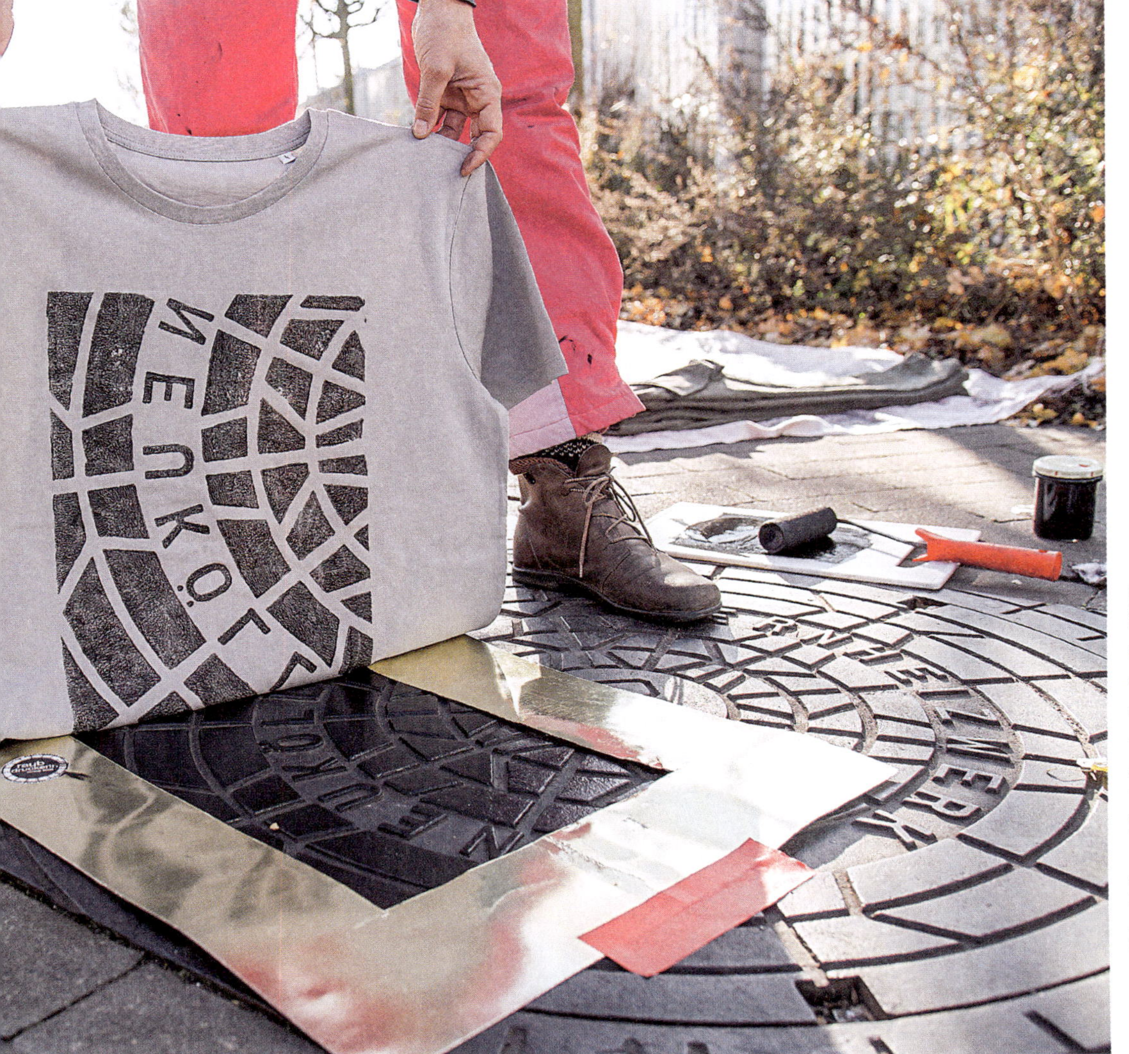

PLANOGRAPHIC PRINTING

BE SPONTANEOUS

Patricia Hardmeier has a background in dance as well as graphic design. Her confident use of colour, combined with a physically expressive process, captures the motion of the clouds. The spontaneity and decisiveness in her mark making create flow, freedom, movement and immediacy, evoking the luminosity and freshness of a windy day. It's all about manipulation: mixing and moving, pushing and pulling the ink around the surface of the plate before committing to taking a print.

On the following pages we will be looking at artists who use planographic printing, which is printing from a flat surface. This monoprint is created as a painting on a glass plate and then a print is lifted directly from it. Moving ink around on a shiny glass surface allows you to wipe areas away to create highlights; smear more inks onto the plate to create shadows or to mix colours; draw marks into the ink to create definition; or decorate the ink with textures, patterns and rhythms of marks.

Monoprinting produces unique images, which capture the joy of expression in a medium that is as fleeting as the sky that Patricia is depicting.

TRY IT YOURSELF

1. Use a shiny surface like a glass plate and silky inks so they will move easily over the surface to allow you to be free with your mark making.

2. Limit your palette of inks. Here, blue and brown are both mixed with white to create all the hues of the sky and land.

3. Use a stiff piece of card to move ink around and to create hard edges. Be purposeful in your mark making, think about the wind blowing and the way the sunlight streams through clouds.

4. Once you are happy, lay the paper on top. Apply pressure evenly to transfer the image, being careful not to move the paper as you press. Lift the paper carefully by two corners of one edge. Lay it out to dry on a clean, flat surface or hang it by two pegs on a line. Do not stack your prints until they are completely dry and no longer tacky to the touch.

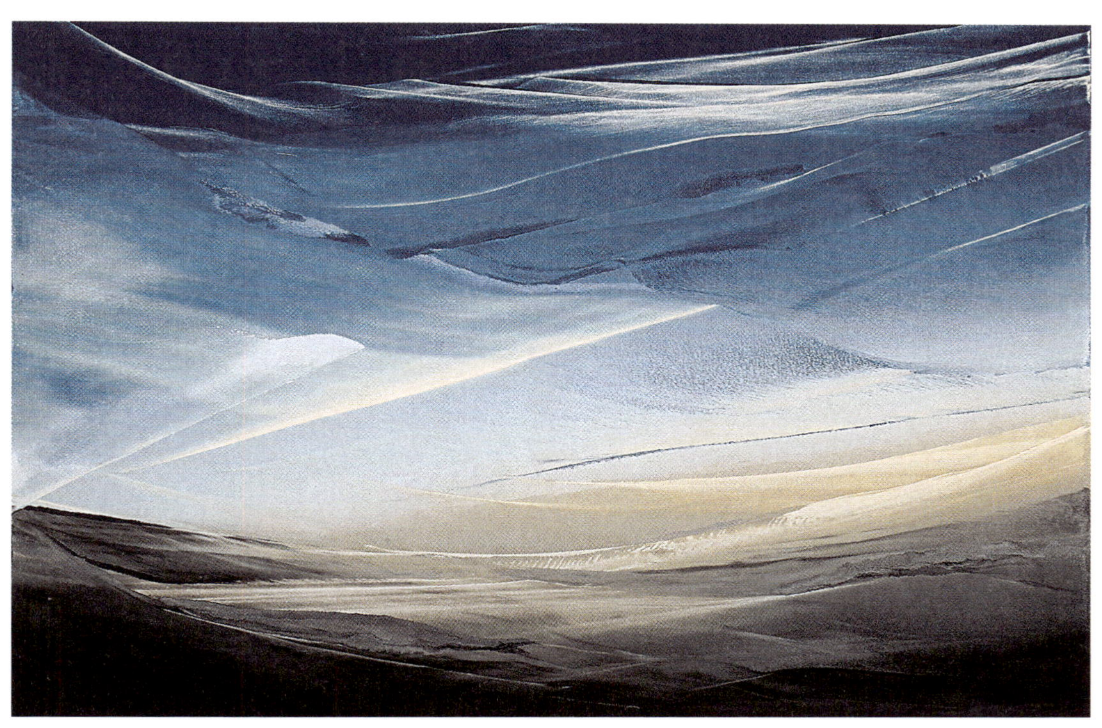

Patricia Hardmeier, *Surrender*, monotype, oil-based ink on rag paper, 2019

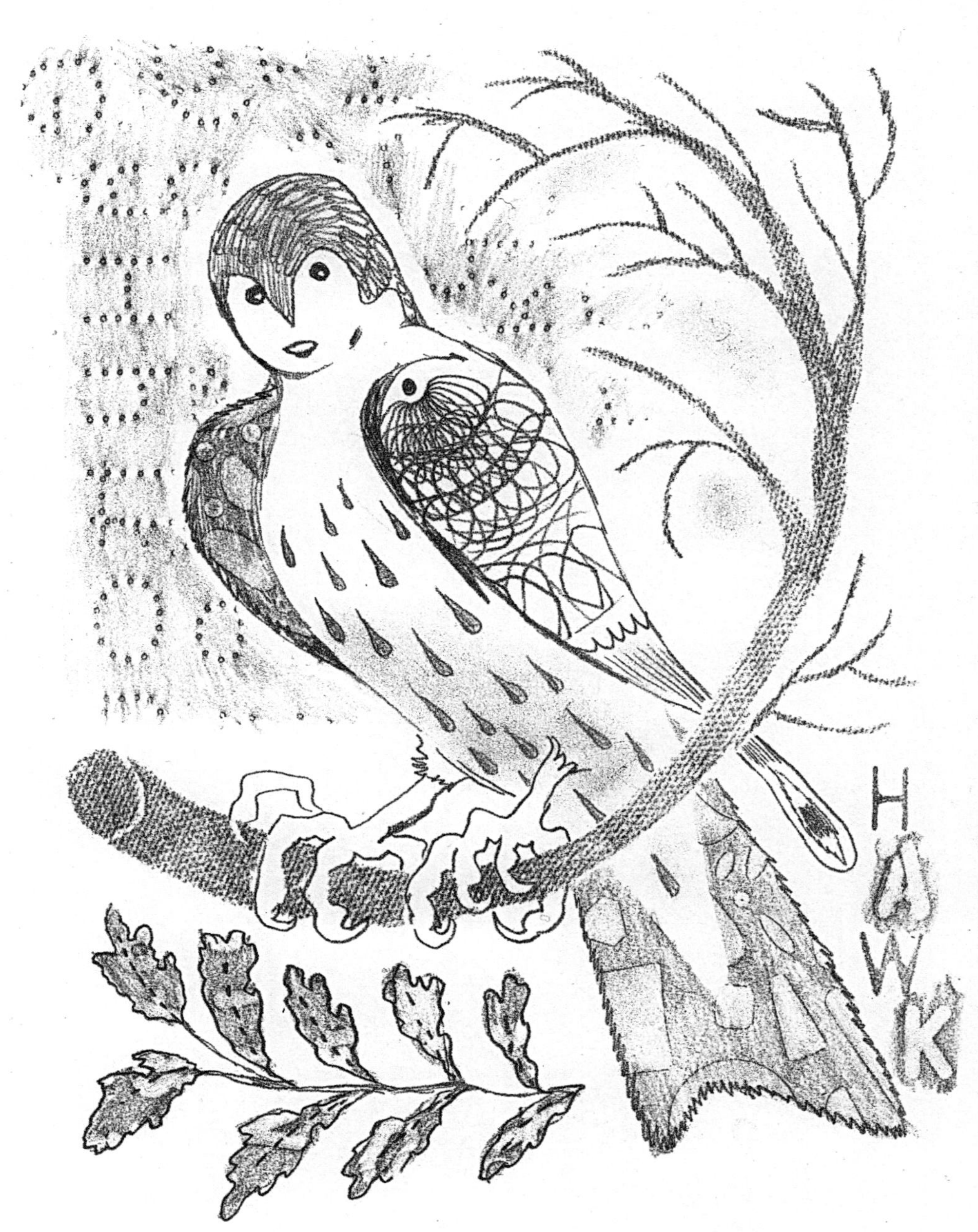
HAWK

MAKE A CARBON COPY

Opposite:
Lily Vie, *Carbon Hawk*, pencil on blue carbon paper and layout paper, 2024

Carbon paper is a thin, waxy paper impregnated with a deep indigo ink used to make copies in the days before photocopying. Lily Vie has used this old stationery staple to create her characterful hawk who looks like she has just flown free from an old English folk ballad. Using a pencil to draw distinct outlines, she has created tonal difference by changing the pressure. Blocks of tone are produced by pressing down on the paper with her finger, and a variety of textures have been introduced by using patterned objects like rough fabric and plastic stencils.

This is called a transfer print because Lily Vie is transferring sections of the carbon ink from the impregnated paper onto her printing surface by applying pressure to the reverse (uninked) side of the carbon paper. This allows her to create a one-off print which has a lovely softness to the drawn line. The print also has a cohesive colour scheme which is formed from the tonal differences of that distinctive indigo colour which is so typical of carbon paper. The monochrome nature of this print gives it a tonal cohesion.

TRY IT YOURSELF

1. Lay the carbon paper face down on top of your printing paper and your drawing paper on top of that. Using a pencil or pen, make your drawing or trace over an earlier drawing.

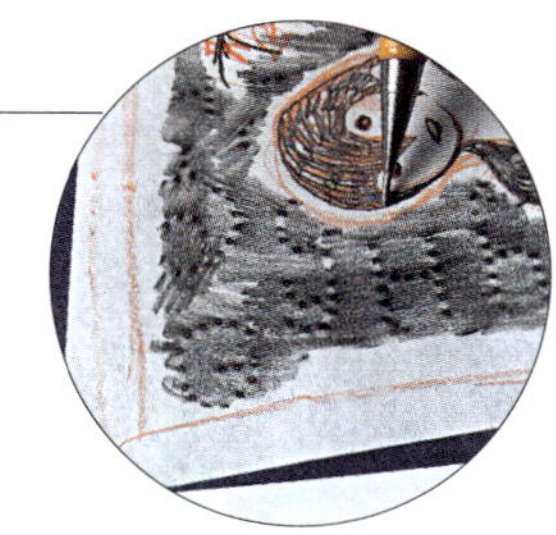

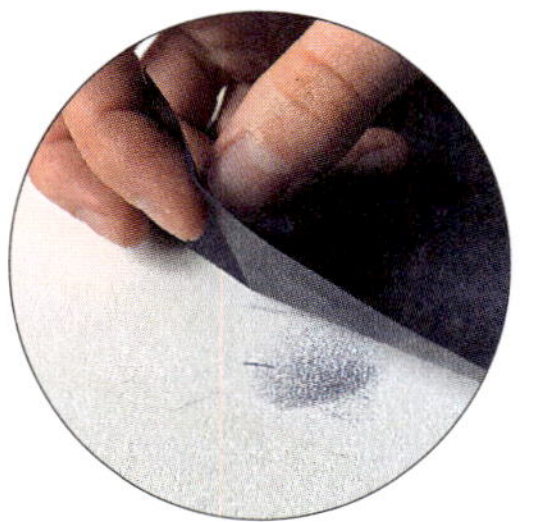

2. If you want to add tone, apply pressure by rubbing with your finger.

3. To add patterns, experiment with placing textured surfaces below the printing paper and then rubbing areas of the drawing so that the carbon paper transfers this texture to the print.

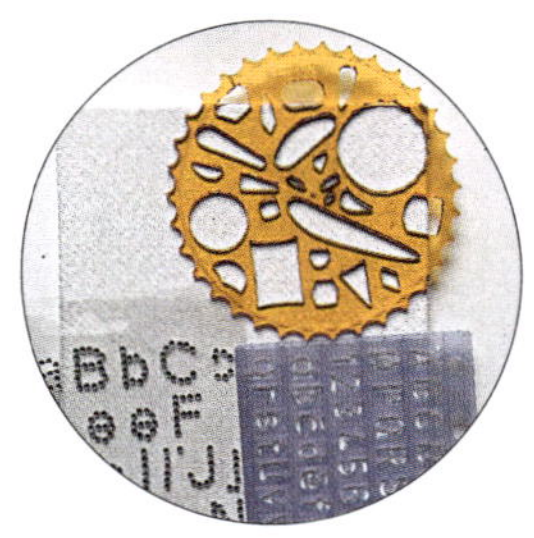

INK UP AND DRAW

Georgina Bown creates large prints of wonderfully characterful submarines. The angle at which she places these submersibles, and the negative space that she allows around them in her composition, communicates the feeling of the immensity and the presence of these huge ships. The areas of tone she creates suggest shadows which gives the submarines form. But, more than that, the tone evokes a sense of that otherworldly underwater light as the submarines hang in the deep-sea gloom.

This form of monoprinting is very close to the carbon-paper technique. To create this printed drawing, Georgina Bown places her paper on top of an inked-up printing plate and then makes her drawing on the back of the paper, being careful to apply pressure only to the areas where she wants to pick up the ink. After she has created the outline, she picks up textured blocks of tone by applying pressure with her fingers. Only once she is happy that she has created the image that she wants, will she peel the paper from the plate revealing the print. The colour is added in paint washes afterwards, once the print is dry.

TRY IT YOURSELF

1. Apply a thin layer of ink to your printing plate. It may take you a few attempts to get the amount of ink correct.

2. Place your paper on top.

3. Remembering that the image will be reversed on the final print, carefully draw your design on the back of the paper. Try not to lean on the paper as you draw.

4. Apply pressure by rubbing the drawing on the areas where you want to create tone.

5. Carefully lift the print by two corners and lay it out to dry.

6. Once it is dry, you can work into the print using other media like paint and coloured pencil.

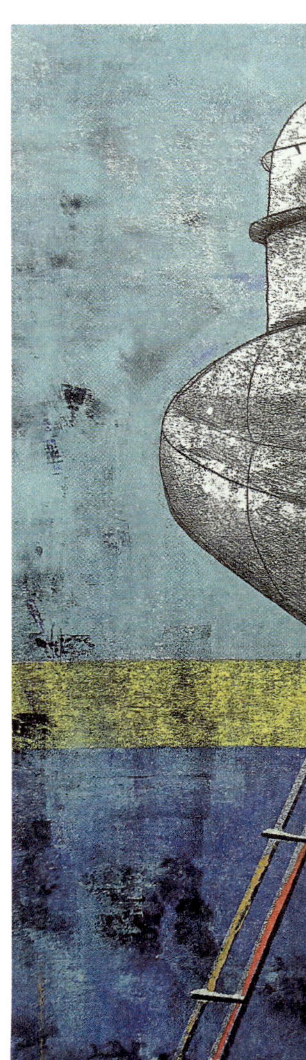

Georgina Bown, *Sub-Stitution 2*, monotype, oil-based ink on paper, 2022

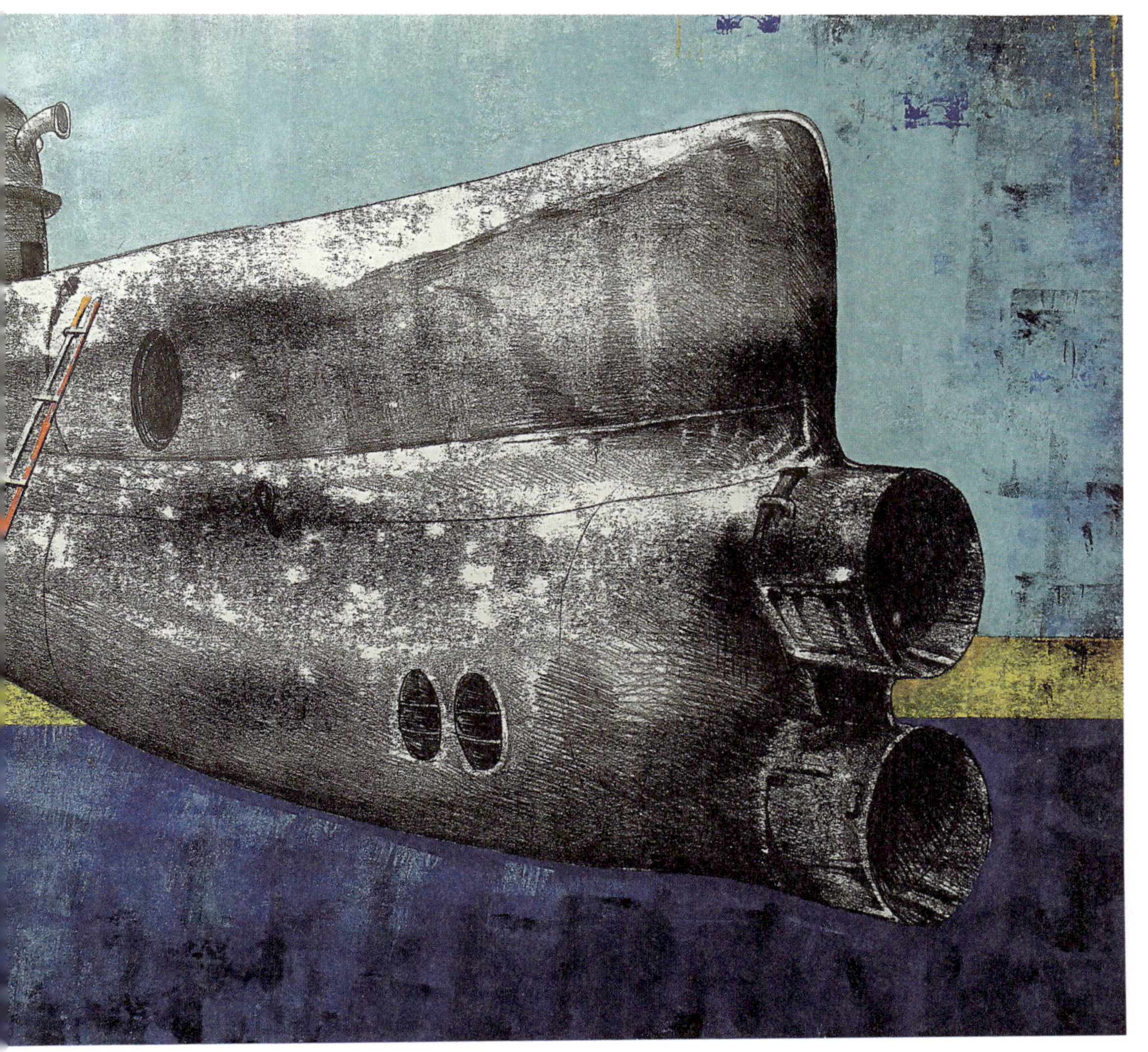

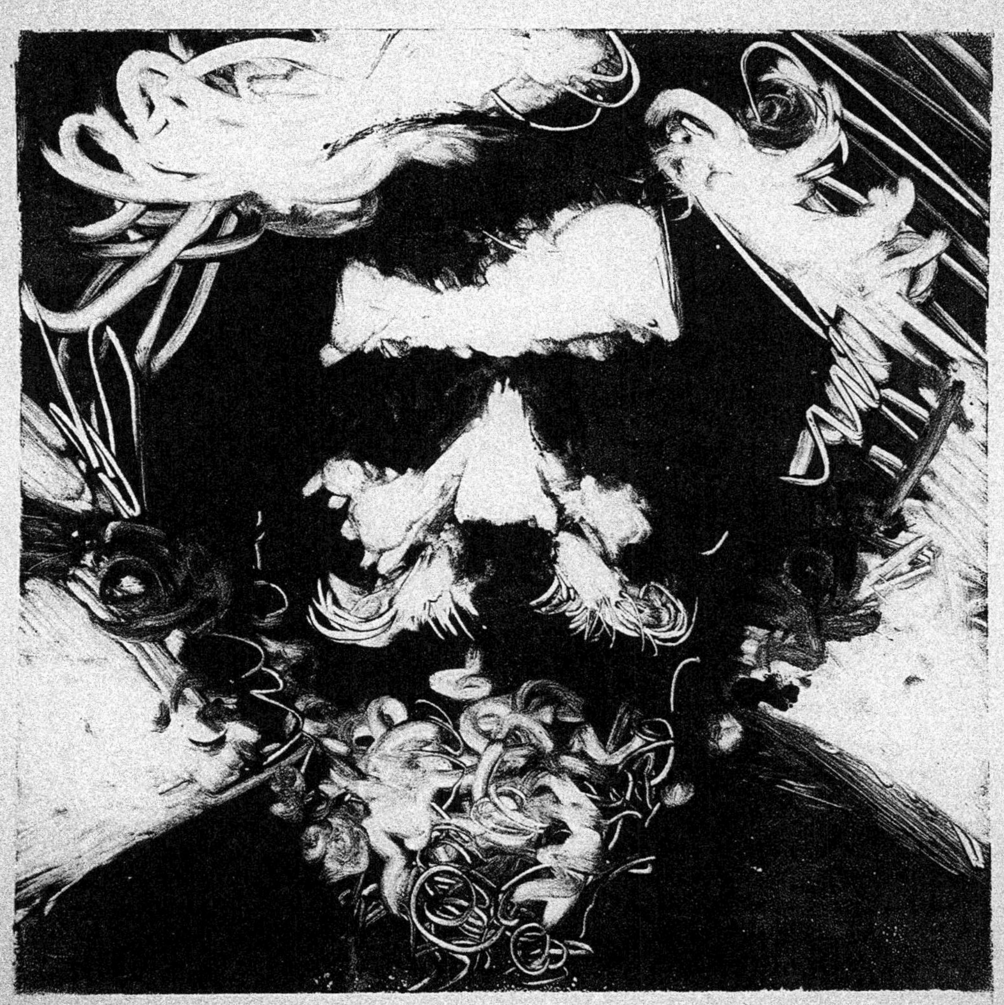

PAINT AND PRINT

Thomas Shahan's self-portrait is an excellent example of why you might choose to make a monoprint. Look at those sumptuous, swooshy lines swirling about to form his beard, those jagged zigzags around his head, those bold inky shadows that describe his heavy brow and the delicate, scratchy lines worming around the edges of his moustache. The portrait is a celebration of mark making and freedom, and monoprinting is the perfect printing process to capture all of this

Monoprinting is a quick process - one of the fastest of all the printing techniques - which lends itself to capturing the energy, variety and spontaneity of the marks that can be made on an inky surface. You can see Thomas Shahan has used his fingers, as well as a sharper tool, to produce a range of marks that create pattern, texture and form. Most of all, these marks build a vitality that gives the print a liveliness and reflects the sitter's character.

TRY IT YOURSELF

1. Apply printing ink to a clean, shiny surface like a sheet of glass or acetate.

2. Use a variety of mark-making tools to create your image. You might like to use your fingertips, a brush, sticks of various sizes and sharpness, and maybe a rag to clear larger areas.

3. Place your printing paper on top of the inky plate and apply even pressure to the back of the paper to transfer the ink onto the paper.

4. Lift to reveal your print.

Opposite: Thomas Shahan, *Self Portrait*, monotype, ink on paper, 2010

REDISCOVER POTATO PRINTING

This mesmerising print has endlessly fascinating motifs that repeat in a pleasing rhythm as our eye travels around the circular composition. Delicate frosty patterns and ghostly shapes emerge out of the cold blues and greys of a winter's fog. It is hard to believe that this potato print is one of the most basic forms of printing, but the artist's method is far from simple. Tracy Simpson cuts potatoes into premeasured squares and rectangles, decorates their faces, then makes hundreds of small prints to build up this complex surface. She controls the image by limiting her colour palette; by working onto a precisely pencilled grid; and by using paper stencils to create clean curves that echo the circular shape of the print. This means that the complexity of the image does not become overwhelming and slide into visual chaos.

TRY IT YOURSELF

1. Get a good-sized Russet potato and cut it to make a smooth surface. Either keep the potato's shape or trim to your desired dimensions. Be sure to blot the potato's face to get rid of excess moisture.

2. Put a small amount of acrylic paint on a palette (straight from the tube or a mix of colours) and brush a thin coat onto the potato's face, being careful to clean the edges to reduce any smudging. Next, press the potato onto a textured surface, such as a fabric like lace, or a dried leaf or flower, which creates a pattern on the painted face.

3. Then, using a cut paper stencil to limit the printing area, press the potato firmly onto the paper. This transfers the image of the pattern onto the paper to create the print.

4. Print onto cotton rag paper with tooth to allow the texture details to come through well.

Tip

Limit yourself to a small number of textures per print. Allow these to repeat and rotate. When using a stencil, be sure to make some tests to see how the thickness of the paper works. There can be some bleed-through if the paper is too thin, or rough lines if it is too thick.

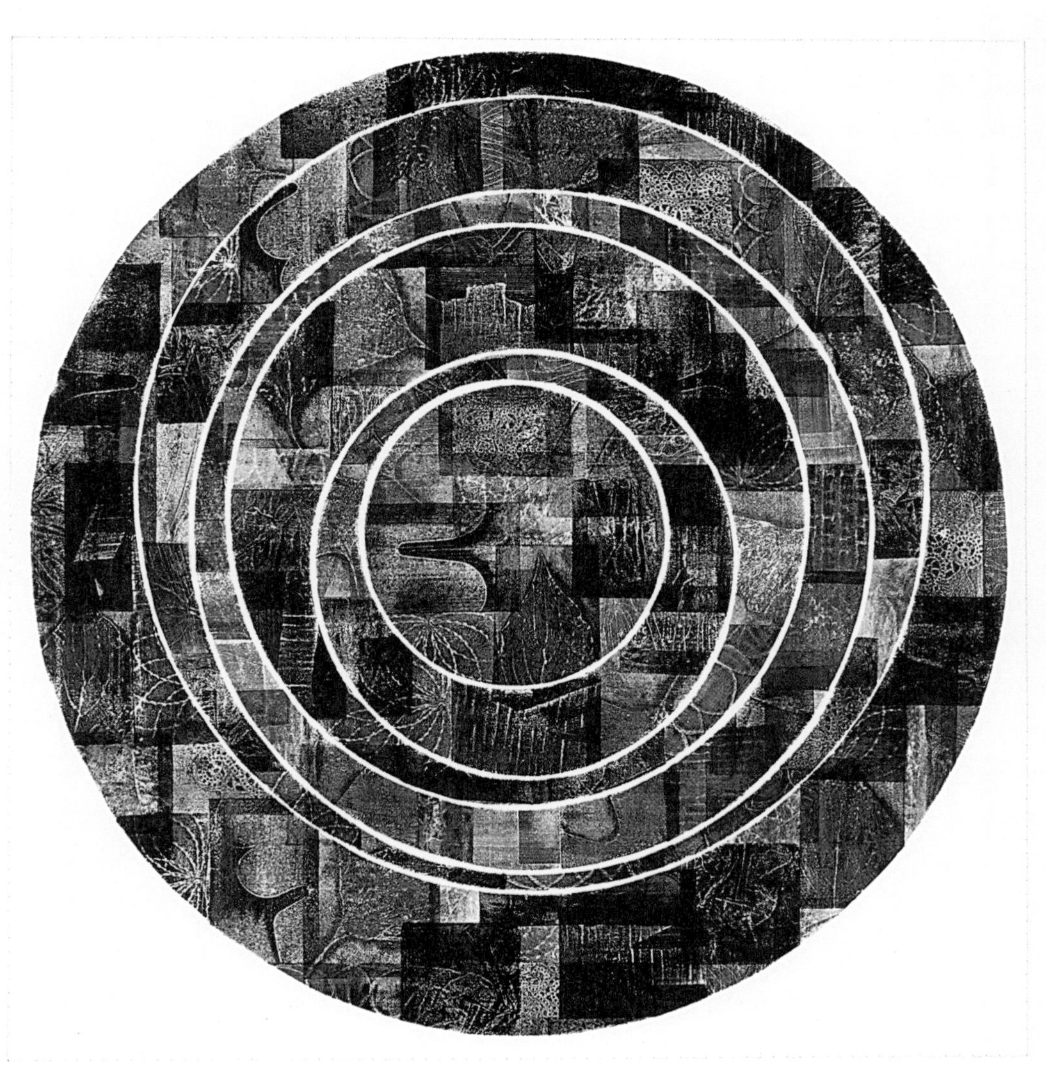

Tracy Simpson, *Day Residu Enso*, monotype print, pencil and acrylic on cotton rag paper, 2021

EMBELLISH WITH COLLAGE

Jane Ormes' prints of decorated horses remind me of the sacred symbols that Native American riders painted on their war horses to give them spiritual power. The starbursts on this horse's rump could symbolize its speed, while the dots of orange near its head might indicate its intelligence. Traditional patterns can be a rich source of inspiration when you are struggling for ideas.

To make this monoprint, the ink on the printing plate is decorated with marks and stamped shapes. Then, before taking the print, a stencil cut in the outline of a horse is placed onto the printing plate. The printing paper is placed on top and pressure applied to transfer the print. The stencil limits the area on which the paper will be printed, defining the edge of the horse. Once the print is dry, it is further embellished using collaged paper shapes, in similar or contrasting colours, to bring an energy and variety of shape and texture to the final piece. Adding the collaged elements allows the introduction of crisp, sharp edges and a variety of complex shapes which complement the soft, blended colours of the monoprint.

TRY IT YOURSELF

Analogous colours

One of the most pleasing aspects of Ormes' horse is the complex variety of analogous hues of blues and greys that she chooses. This gives the piece a good deal of variety, but creates a palette of kindred, or analogous, colours. Analogous colours sit next to each other on the colour spectrum and create a calm harmony when used together.

Complementary colours

Here, the collaged shapes are in complementary colours like orange, which, when placed on the blue background, create a zing of visual energy.

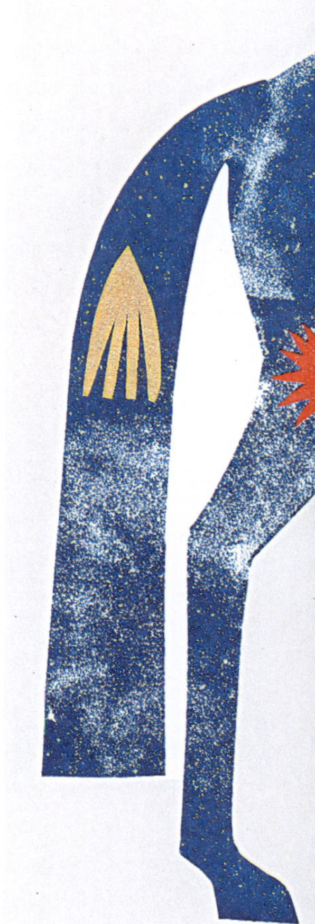

Jane Ormes,
Monoprint Horse,
oil-based inks and
gouache collaged
paper on cotton
paper, 2023

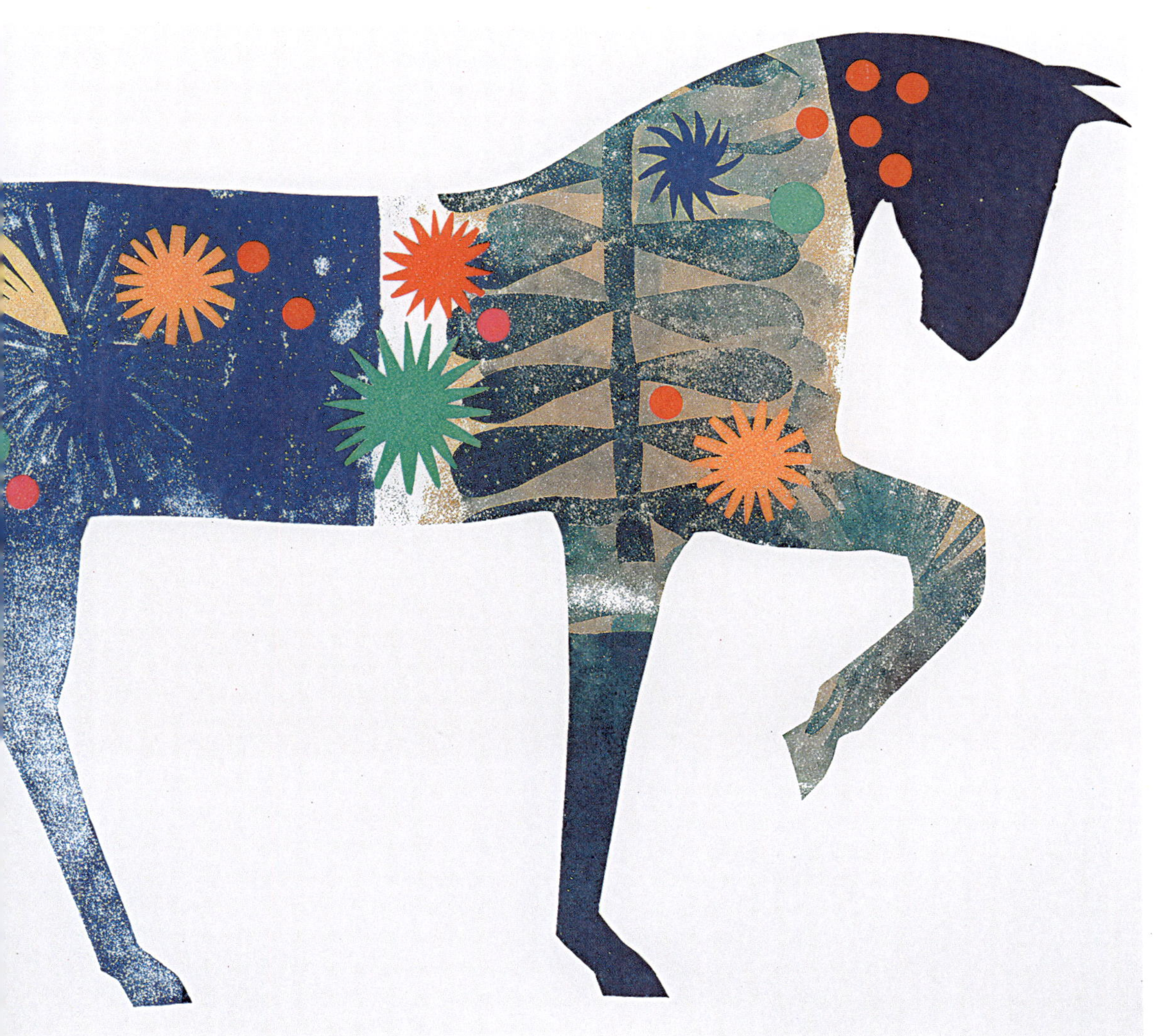

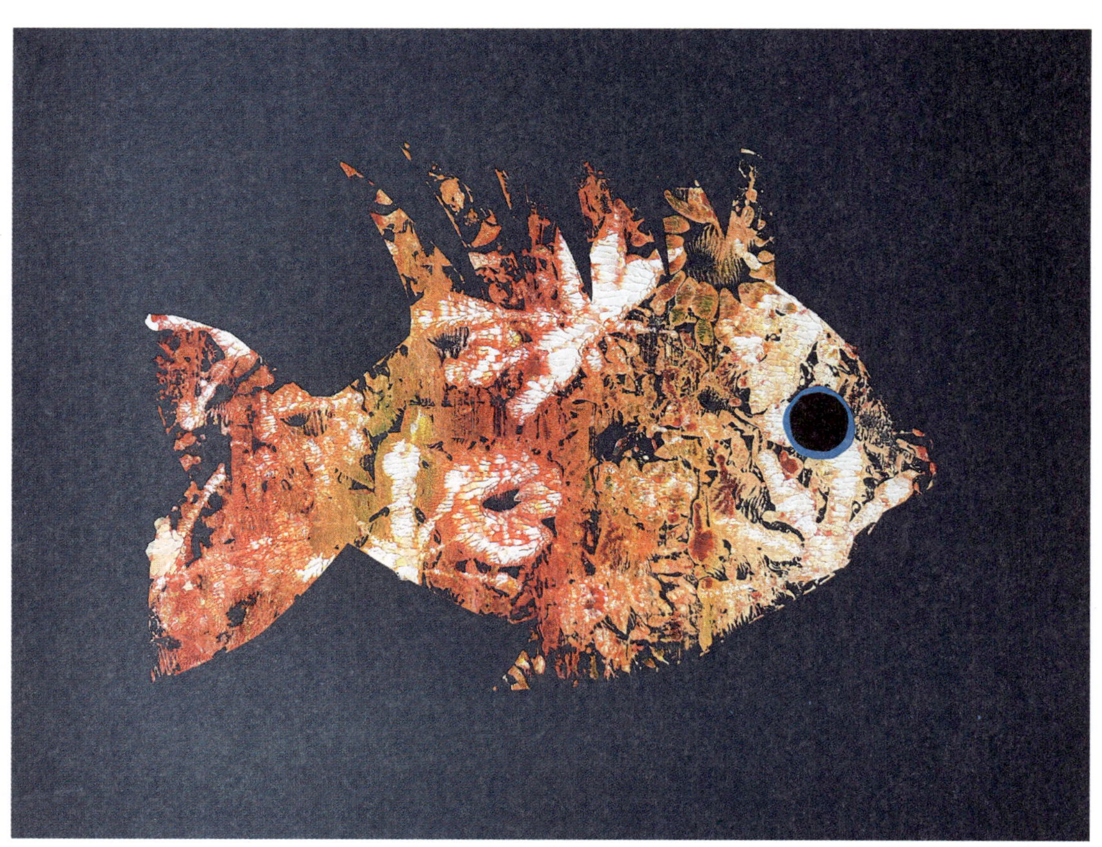

Eve Blackwood, *Goldfish*, monoprint, acrylic paint on coloured paper, 2024

USING STENCILS

Stencils are pieces of paper, card or acetate with holes cut into them that allow paint or ink to pass through. In printing they are used to isolate areas that you want to print by blocking the areas that you don't want to print. This project will demonstrate this in a simple way.

TRY IT YOURSELF

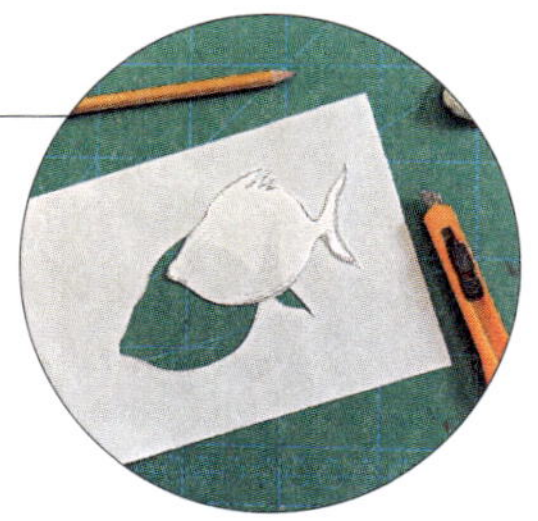

1. Cut the shape of the fish from a piece of paper or thin card, preserving the piece with the fish-shaped hole in it.

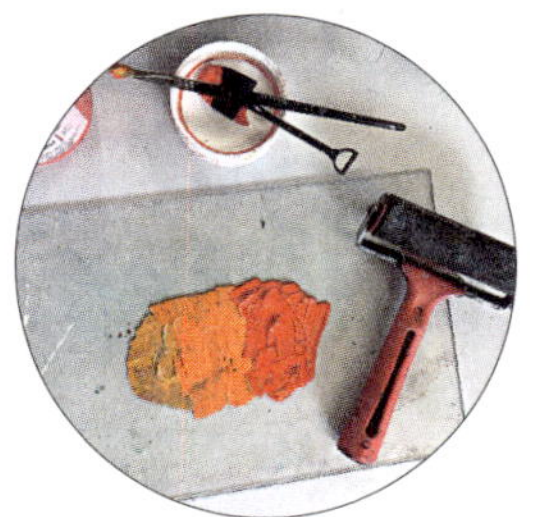

2. Create a colourful, patterned surface of ink on your printing plate. You can do this in a number of ways, but in this example a brayer has been used to mix two colours on the inking plate to create a gradient effect. Then the inky surface has been worked into by drawing with cotton buds, and by stamping different colours of ink on top using shapes cut out of plasticine and small pieces of lino discarded from a larger printing plate.

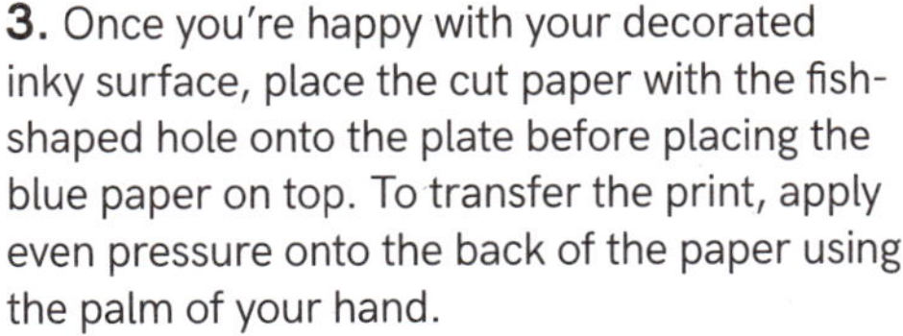

3. Once you're happy with your decorated inky surface, place the cut paper with the fish-shaped hole onto the plate before placing the blue paper on top. To transfer the print, apply even pressure onto the back of the paper using the palm of your hand.

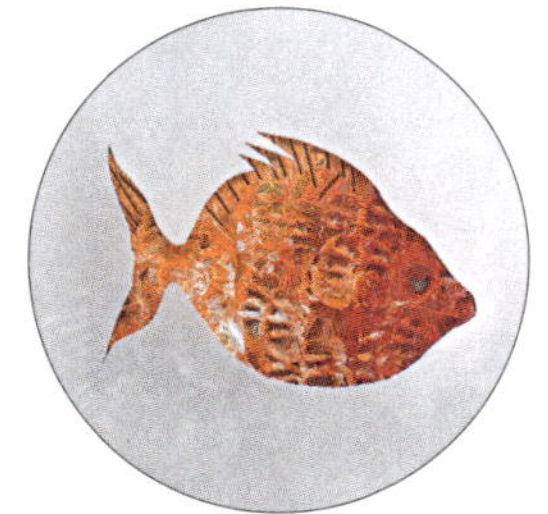

4. Carefully lift the print off, holding it by two corners, and lay it on a clean, flat surface to dry.

Colour temperature

Colour temperature refers to the idea that yellow, orange and red are warm colours while blues and greens are cool colours. Although this is not universally true (you can have warm greens for example), it is a good rule of thumb to bear in mind when planning a colour palette. Cool colours recede while hot colours jump out at you.

LAYER INKS TO CREATE DEPTH

Laura Crehuet Berman's blended colours combine to create this luminous depiction of a polished gemstone. The print evokes crystalline layers and facets catching the light, illuminating a complex fusion of hues in a captivating way. Laura produces this effect by building up layers of colour, while restricting the printing area using lozenge-shaped stencils. Controlling the outline of the print to create a soft curved shape, she evokes the smooth surface of the gem.

There are two reasons for the success of this print. The first is the choice of colour palette: strong jewel colours that are blended with each other to make gradients; the second is the transparency of the inks which allows another level of blending. These gradients overlap, creating harmonious combinations and bringing depth to the image which gives it an opalescent, colour-changing quality.

TRY IT YOURSELF

Gradients

Gradients - also known as colour ramps or colour progressions - describe the process of blending two or more colours so that they gently fade into each other. In printing, a common way of doing this is by using a brayer to roll the colours together in a linear way on the inking palette. After that, you can apply this blend to the printing plate or, as in this case, take a direct print from the rolled mix through a stencil to create a multi-layered monoprint.

Tip

Using a variety of stencils to apply gradients so that they partially overlap will create even more complex combinations of colours. This can bring depth, as well as a sophisticated subtlety, to your prints.

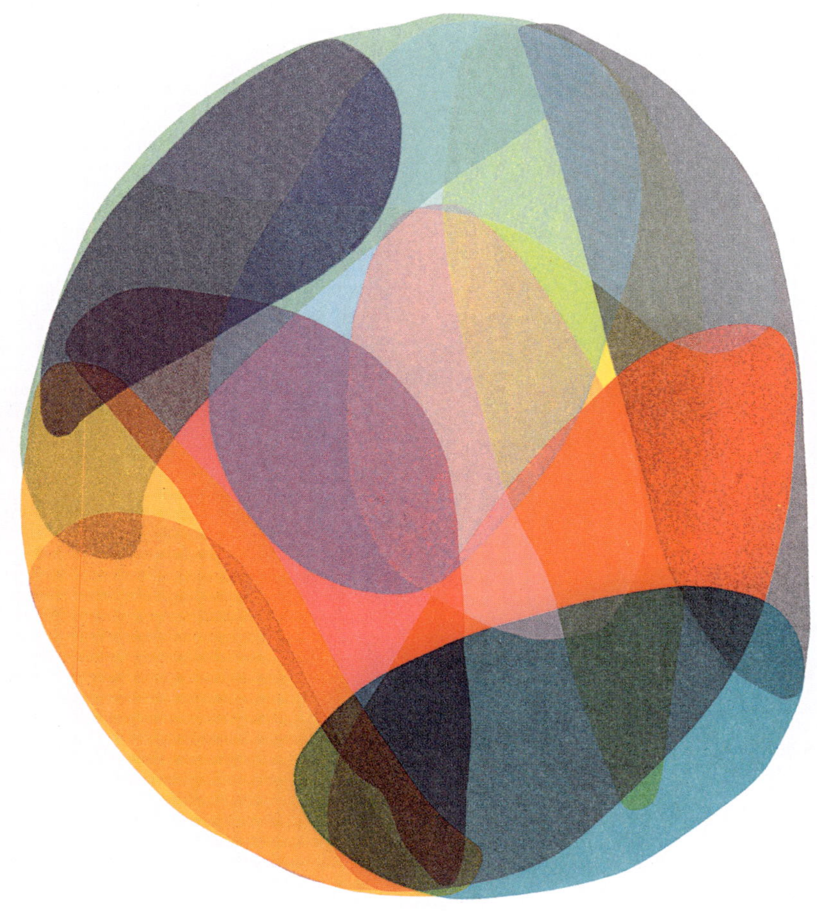

Laura Crehuet Berman, *Gem L7*, monoprint, relief-printing ink on paper, 2021

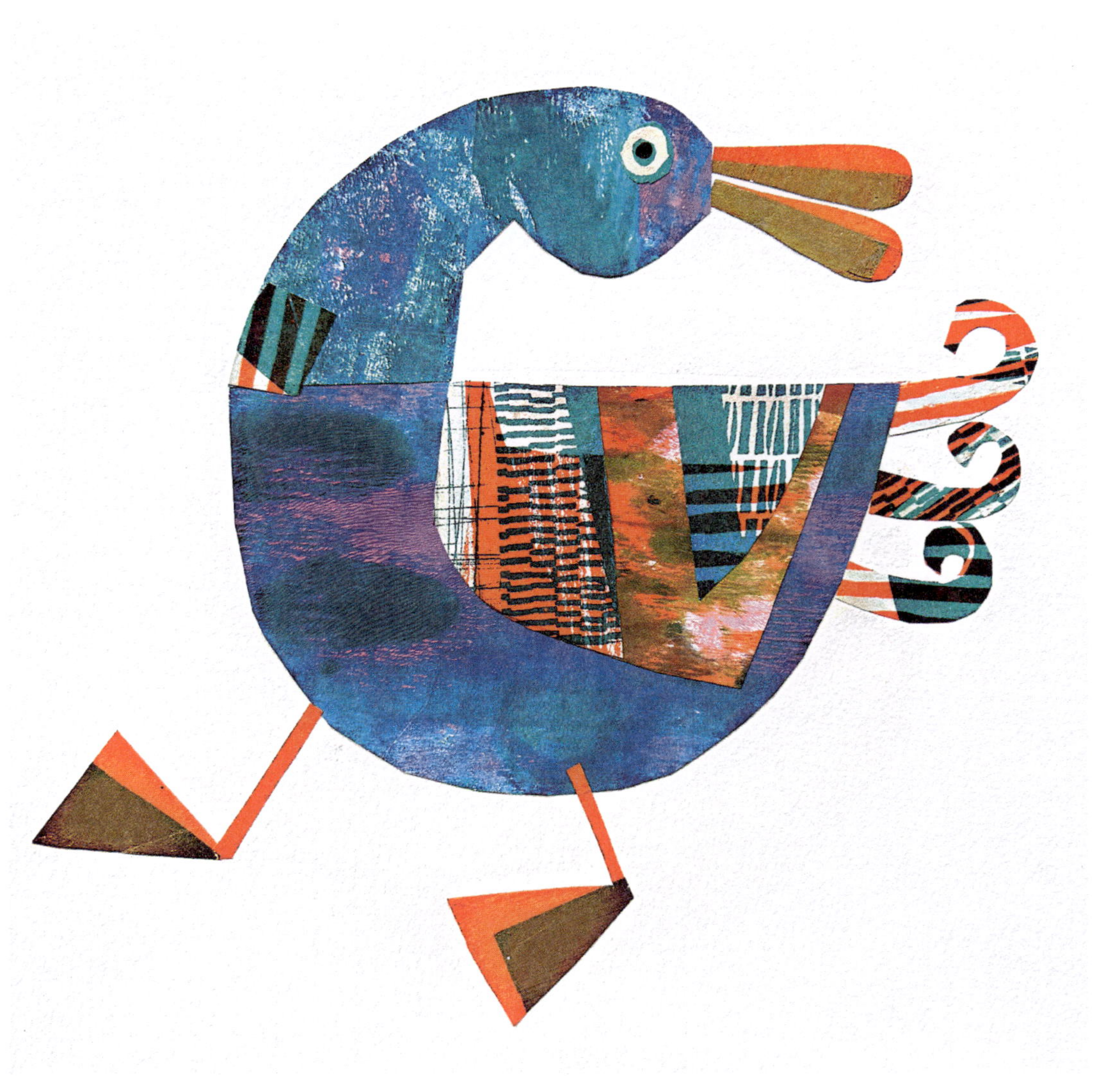

Clare Youngs, *Happy Duck*, Riso print and gelli print, gold leaf and gouache, 2023

GELLI PRINTING

Gelli printing is one of the techniques that Clare Youngs has used to make the colourful and diverse printed papers that she has then collaged together to create her duck. She has created a variety of textures on her Gelli prints by using stencilling and stamping to bring a repeating rhythm to the duck's wings. On the body of the duck she has used a Gelli print built up of layers of rolled paint to create an uneven textured combination of blues, pinks and purples, which suggests the iridescent colours of the duck's feathers. Her use of mainly complementary colours - blue and orange - add to the lively energy of this characterful duck. The simplicity of Clare Youngs' design holds these disparate pieces together in a cohesive way.

TRY IT YOURSELF

This is a great example of how to recycle prints that you might otherwise discard to make a fresh new composition. Test prints, badly registered prints, offcuts or discarded colour experiments are all worth keeping as possible collage material.

Playing with colour combinations or putting together patterns in an experimental collage forces you to make artistic decisions and can help inform your choices when planning your print designs.

Exciting and unexpected things can happen when you start putting your offcuts together in a new way.

GELLI PRINTING EXPLORED

Making small Gelli prints, like these by Lily Vie, is an excellent way to get to grips with this flexible printing method.

Gelli printing works by decorating the surface of a gelatine printing plate through layering up acrylic paint. These layers can be built up to create complex combinations of colour, pattern, line and repeating motifs. It is important to allow the paint to dry on the Gelli plate before applying the next layer.

TRY IT YOURSELF

Here are some ideas of techniques you can experiment with. Remember that any image you create will be reversed when you print it.

Painting
Paint with a brush, draw with acrylic pens or use a roller to apply colour mixes directly onto the printing plate.

Drawing
Use a cotton bud to draw on wet paint by wiping areas clean. This will let the next colour you apply on top show through.

Stencils
Use stencils to limit the edges and to make colourful shapes or roll your paint through a material like lace or fruit netting to create a pattern.

Stamping
Use objects or cut stamps to print patterns onto the plate.

Transfer printing
Try transferring a printed image using a thin layer of paint and a high-gloss image from a magazine.

Check your work
As the Gelli printing plate is clear, you can check your print's progress by looking through the plate from the unpainted side.

Top to bottom
When you work in this way, you are building your print from top to bottom, so the final layer you apply to the plate will become the base colour of the image when you transfer the print onto paper.

Opposite:
Lily Vie, *Assorted Gelli prints*, acrylic paint, magazine pages, textured materials, leaves and collage, 2024

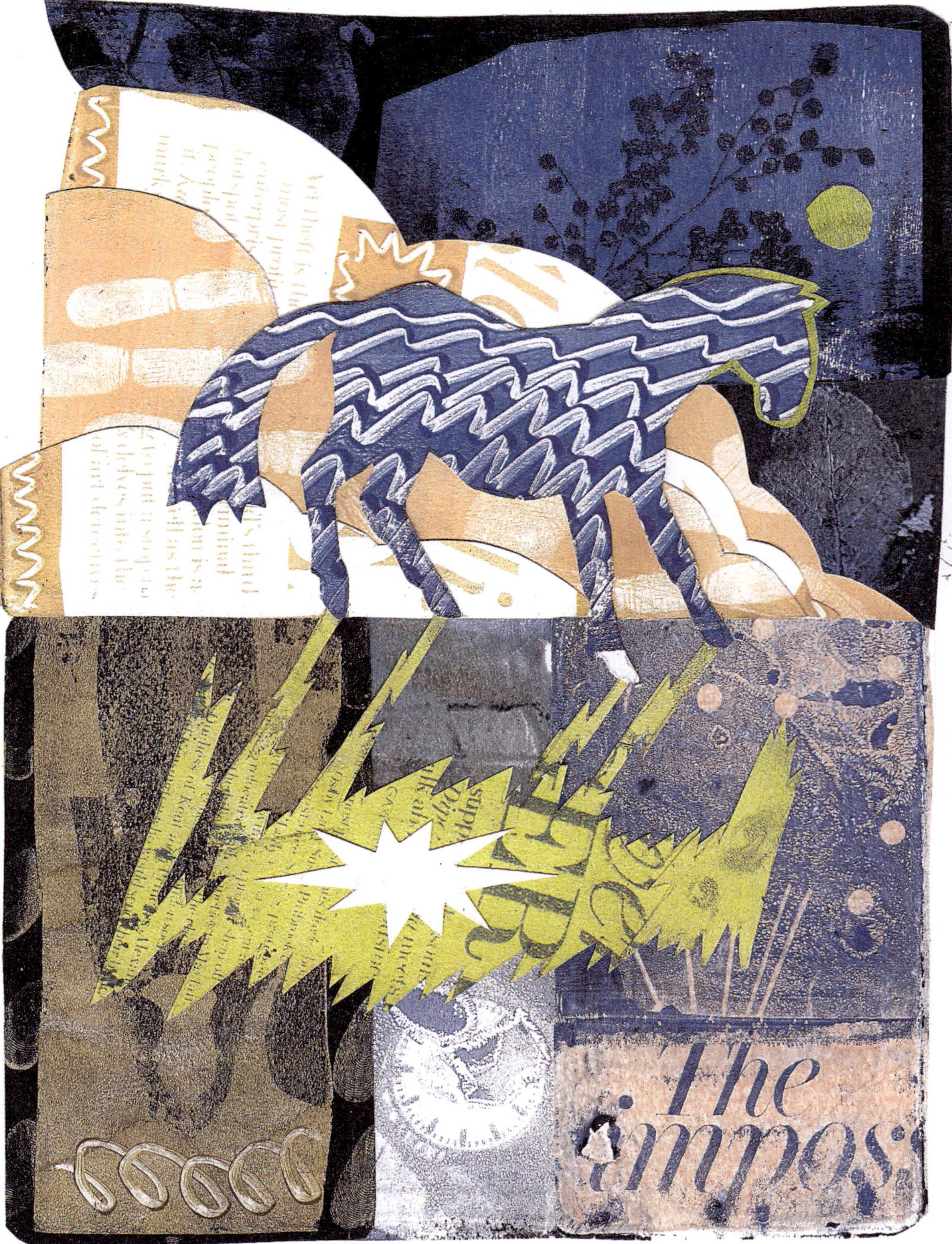
The
impos

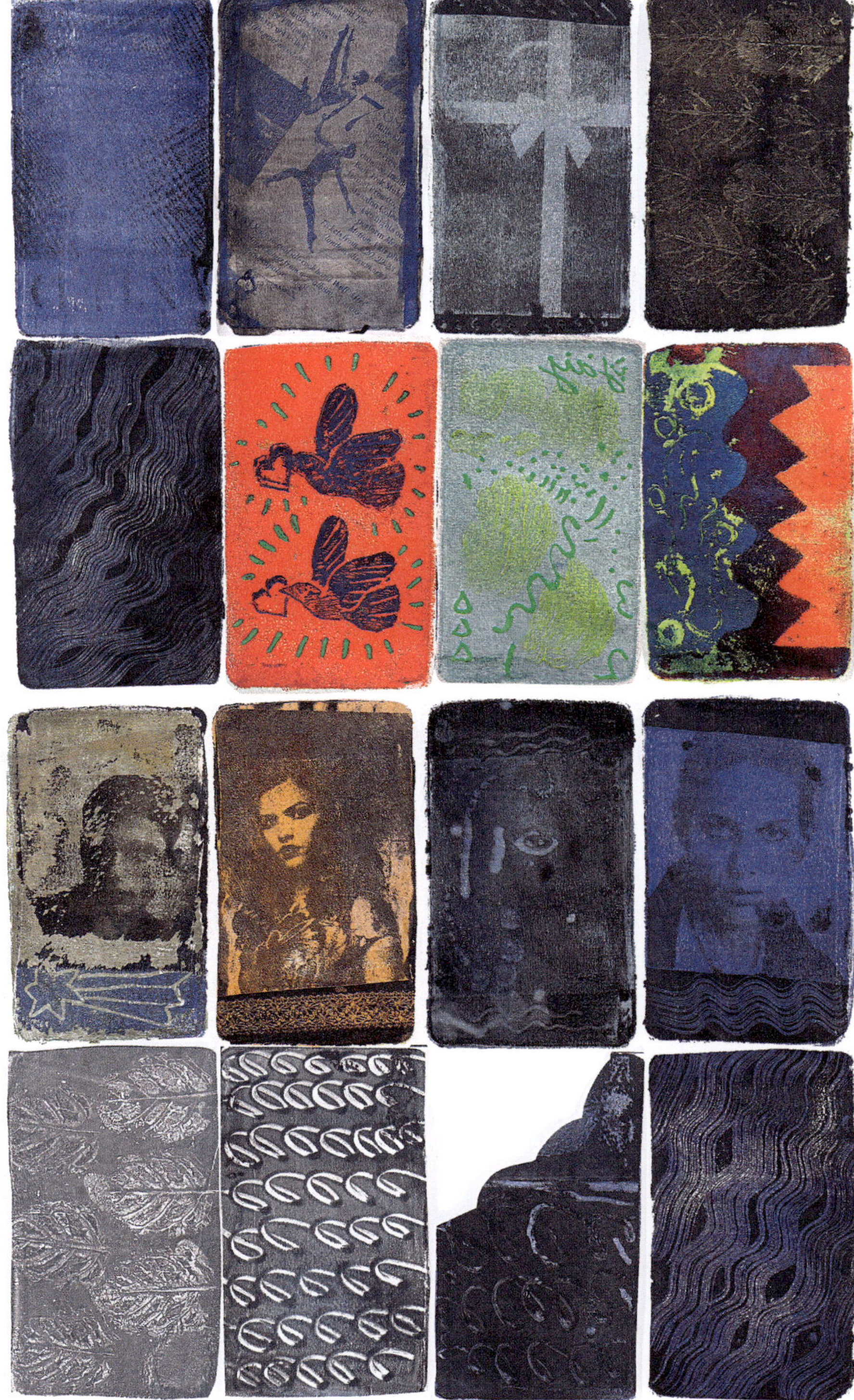

Finishing

Once you are happy with your image, and the paint is dry, you can apply the final background colour on the top of the plate.

Transferring to paper

Transfer the print onto slightly damp paper by laying the paper on the top of the painted Gelli plate followed by a pile of heavy books.

Timings can vary

How long you will need to leave this for the image to fully transfer to the paper depends on how damp the paper is and how warm the air temperature is. This will be trial and error when you first start. Keep checking the print transfer by lifting the corner of the paper to see if the image has stuck.

Tip

Once you have taken the print, the Gelli plate can then be washed and used again.

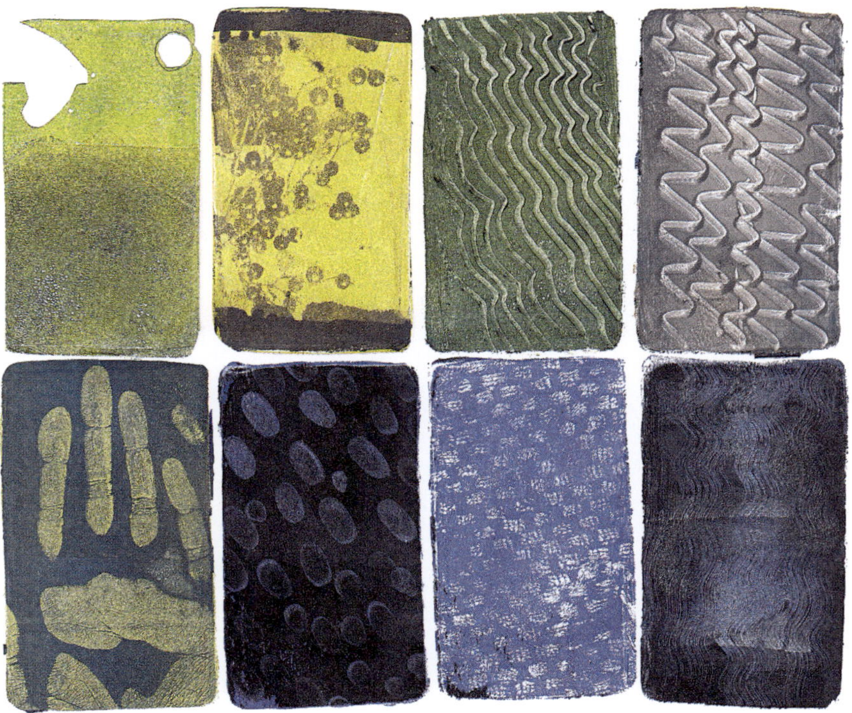

Lily Vie, *Assorted Gelli prints*, acrylic paint, magazine pages, textured materials, leaves and collage, 2024

RELIEF PRINTING

BRING YOUR SUBJECT TO LIFE

In this section of the book, we will be looking at artists who make relief prints. The big message of relief printing is that mark making is king. It creates form, texture, pattern and visual interest, and is a conduit for the artist's creative expression.

This lino print by Rachel Newling is a great example of the wide variety of detail that a printmaker can achieve through mark making. The surface of this bird is so cleverly described that we can imagine what it would feel like to touch. The repeating motif of the individual feathers build and morph to create the complex texture of the bird's body, while the different weights of line create definition and depth. This print has been hand-coloured with complementary colours to introduce pattern and highlights. Rachel is thoughtful in her approach to clearing the empty area of negative space behind the bird, allowing room for our eye to settle, but also leaving enough of a trace of the carving lines to add energy to the overall composition. The final effect is a vibrant print which captures the exotic beauty, character and rich colour of the subject.

TRY IT YOURSELF

Think about texture
Look closely at the surfaces and textures of the scene that you would like to depict. Choose a combination of marks that suggest the feel of that surface.

Descriptive mark making
Think about varying the scale of the marks you make. Smaller marks can appear further away, adding depth to your image.

Inspiration
Look at Vincent Van Gogh's ink drawings: they are a great source of inspiration for expressive mark making.

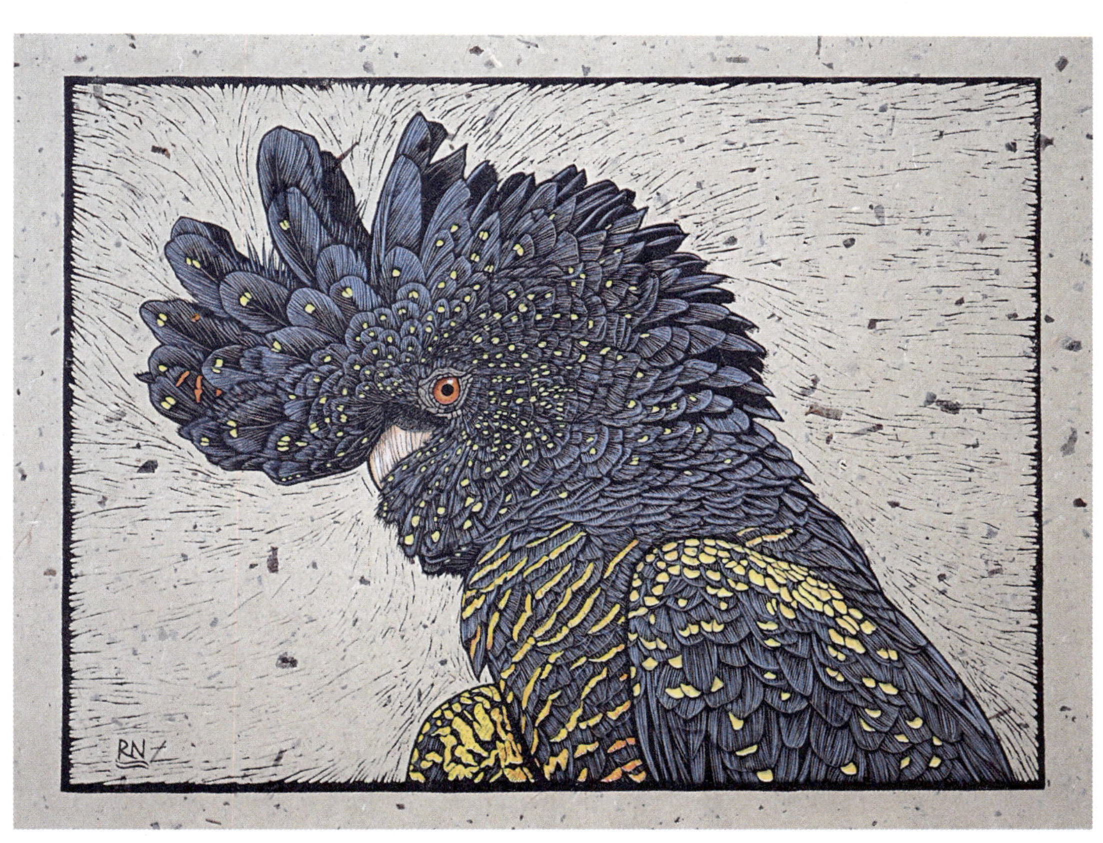

Rachel Newling, *Red Tailed Black Cockatoo Portrait*, linocut on Japanese washi paper, 2014

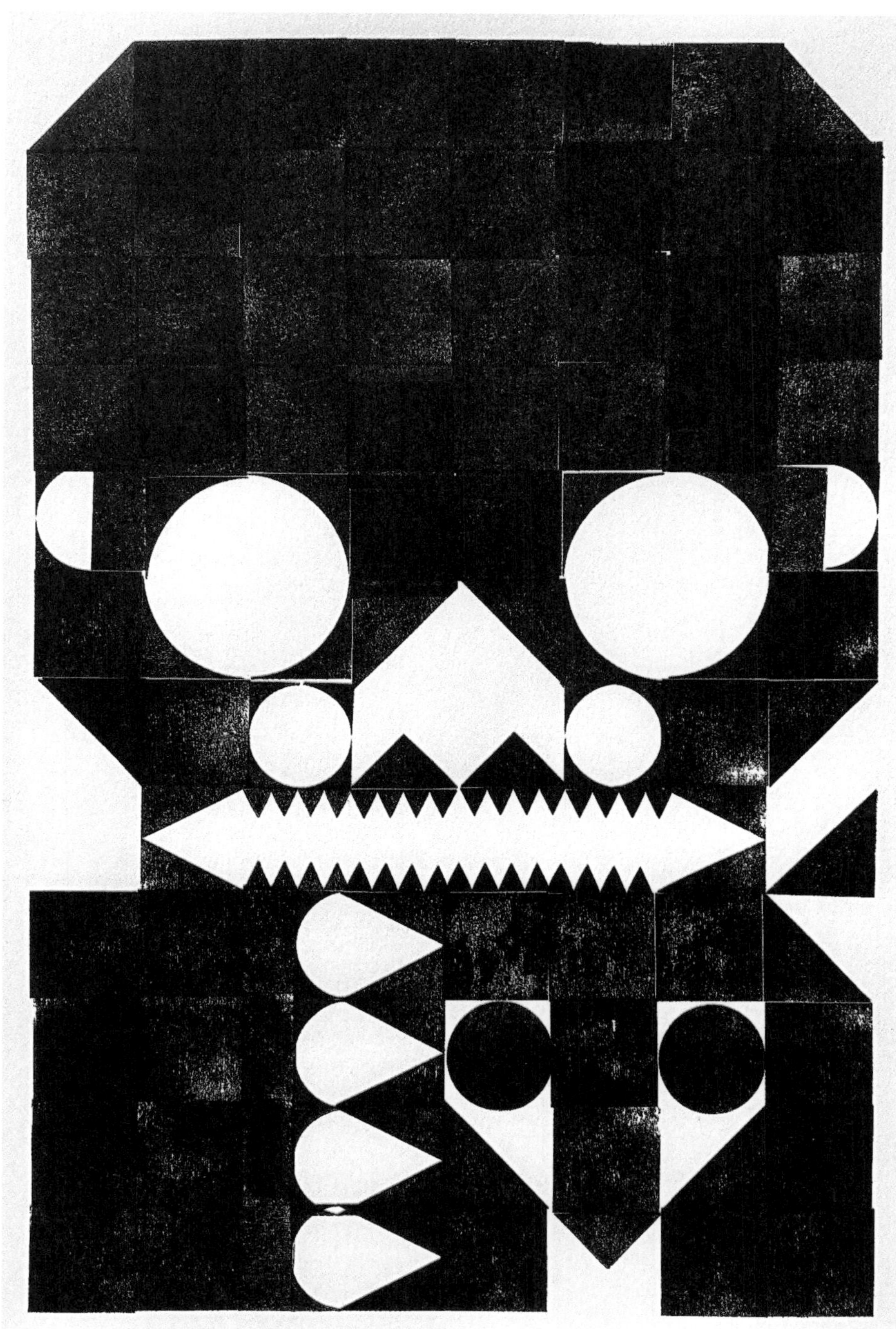

Paul Farrell, *Beowulf*, relief print, ink-pad ink on paper, 2023

CREATE A CHARACTER WITH STAMPS

'Out from the marsh, from the foot of misty hills and bogs, bearing God's hatred, Grendel came ...' *Beowulf*

Grendel is a pagan monster who is slain by the eponymous hero of *Beowulf*, an epic poem written in Old English 1000 years ago. Paul Farrell creates a textured block of darkness from which the troll-like face emerges full of gnashing teeth and pointed talons, crafted from the stark, unprinted white of the paper. This dark and imposing monster is created using 16 bespoke shapes and a squared grid. The individual prints are made from carved rubber stamps, using black ink on white paper. Its simple blockiness suits the elemental nature of the subject.

This printing method is the simplest form of relief printing: stamps. The 16 shapes have been ingeniously combined to depict Grendel. He is pieced together in the way we might construct him from a set of wooden building blocks. By limiting yourself to a few shapes, you and your audience will have to use their imaginations to flesh out the printed image.

TRY IT YOURSELF

Make a stamp

Stamps like these can be made from carving rubber erasers.

Draw your design

Draw your shape onto the surface of the eraser then, using a sharp craft knife, cut down the surrounding rubber to leave the shape as a raised surface on the stamp.

Inking up

Rather than try to ink these up with a roller, you might find it easier to use an ink pad to press them into before printing them onto the paper.

Inspiration

Characters from literature have long been a rich source of inspiration for artists. Perhaps you could challenge yourself to interpret one in print.

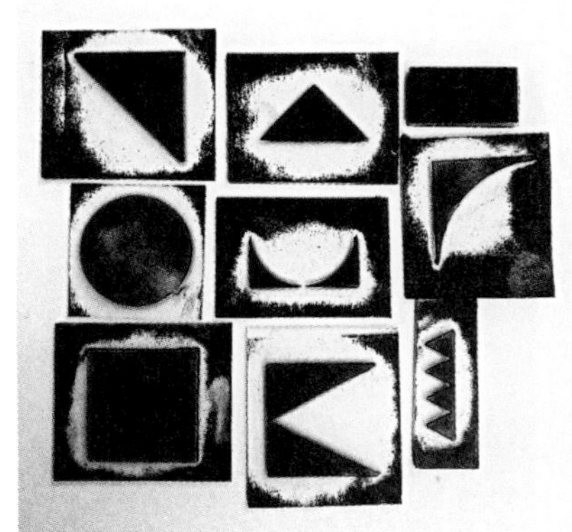

Rubber stamp shapes used to create *Beowulf*

CARVE A BOLD DESIGN

Opposite: Asimina Hollingworth, *Beatnik*, potato print, relief-printing ink on paper, 2024

Ah, the humble potato, starchy stalwart of the dinner plate! But what about its potential as a printing medium? We have already seen that, in its raw state and sliced straight down its belly, the potato becomes a smooth surface that can be used to transfer decorated ink onto a printing surface. But its potential does not end there. A potato is also a versatile medium when you approach it in the way that we did as children, as a stamp that can be carved.

Asimina Hollingworth has leaned into the repetitive nature of stamping by building up repeating patterns and textures to bring rhythm and a little chaos to her beatnik's hair. She uses the natural shape of the potato to dictate the shape of his eyes, which stare at us with fierce intensity. His character is generated by the character of the printing medium.

TRY IT YOURSELF

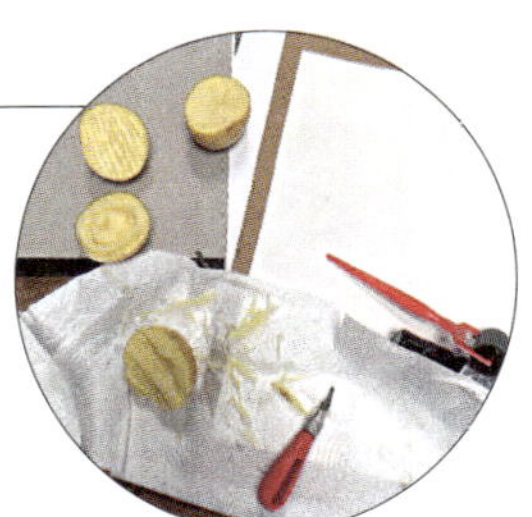

Work with the medium
The key to a successful print with such a simple process is to limit your colours and embrace the character of the medium.

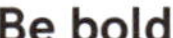

Be bold
Potatoes don't lend themselves to fine, fiddly cuts, so stick to bold designs.

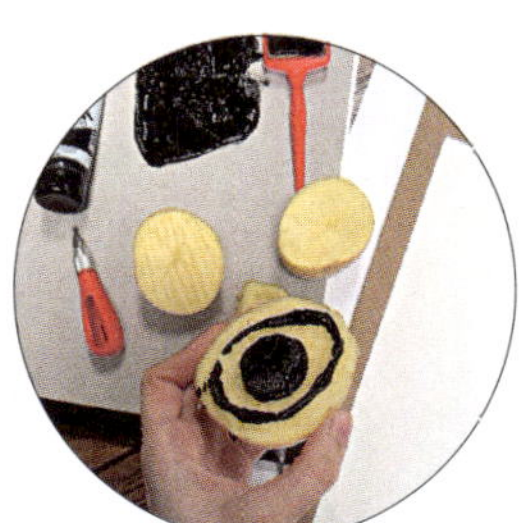

Carving
You can use a sharp knife or linocutting tools to carve the surface of the halved potato and create your printing stamps.

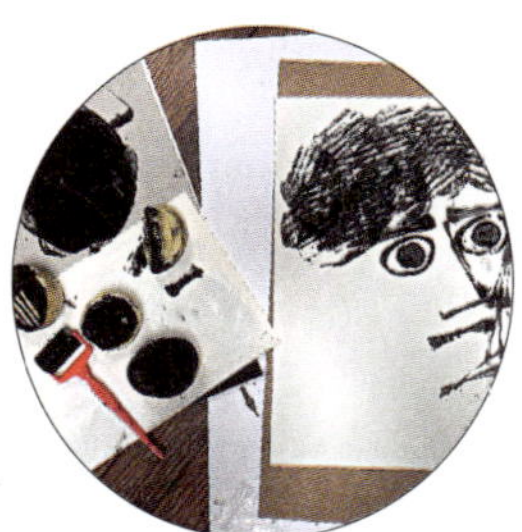

Inking up
Relief-printing ink or acrylic paint are good choices for this medium.

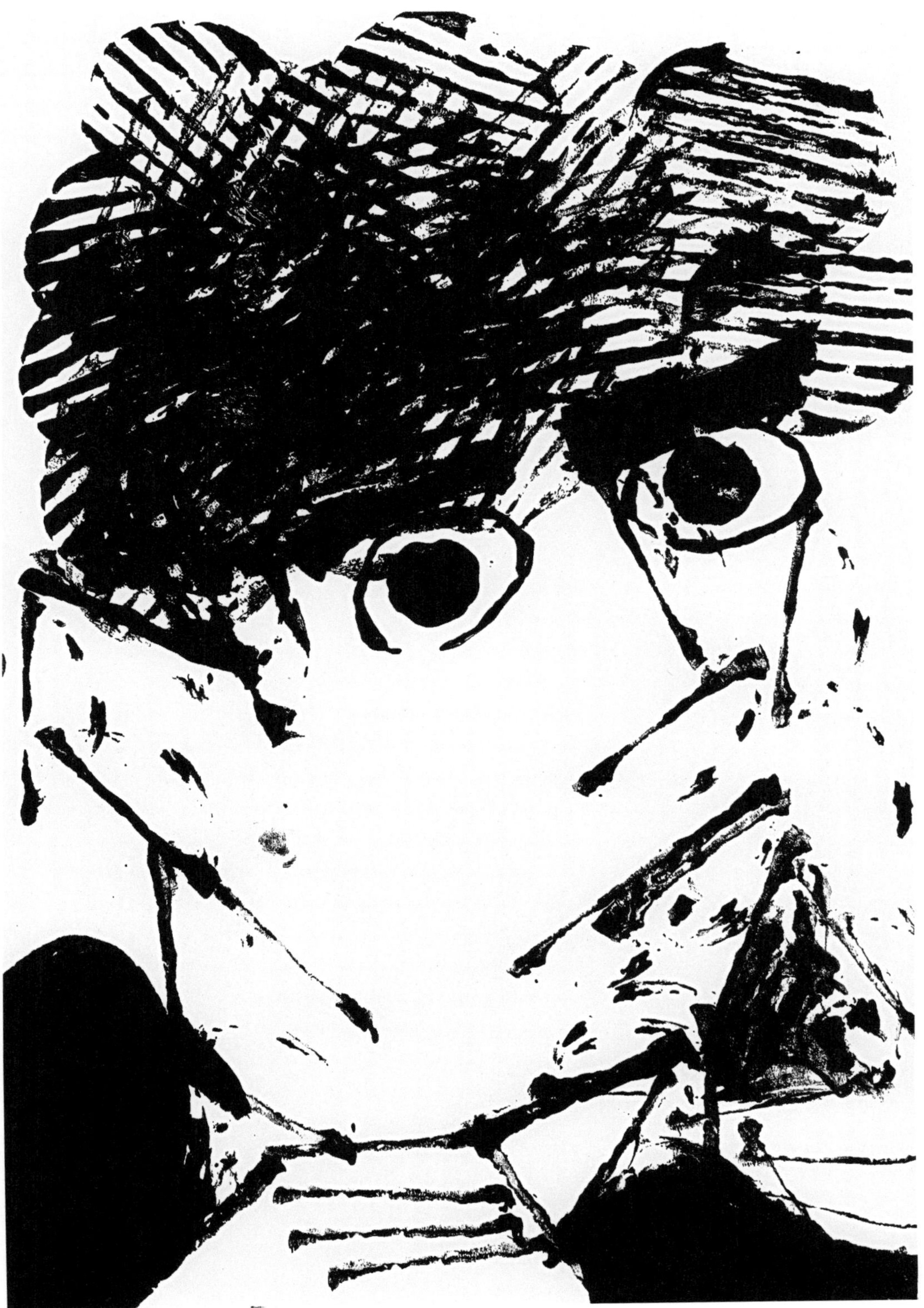

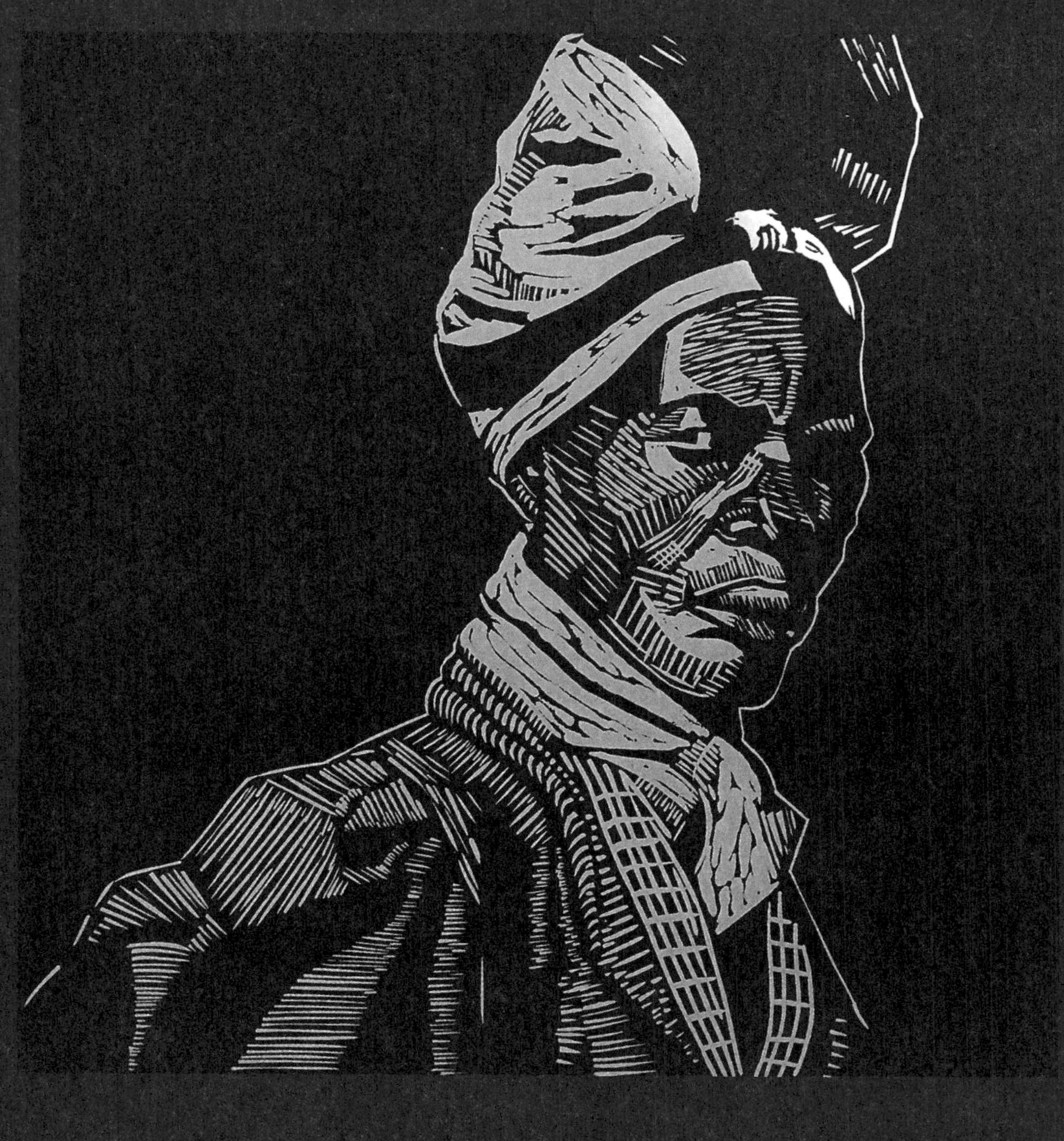

USE HIGH CONTRAST TO ADD DRAMA

LaToya Hobbs' masterful use of light and dark gives power to her formidable subject. The marks she carves into the lino convey a variety of information. There are marks that tell us about the structure of the jacket, the pattern on the collar and the texture of the scarf. Other lines describe the contours of the woman's face and create that intimidating look in her eye, challenging us to engage with her. What all these lines are doing is describing where the light is falling on her. This is dramatic lighting: she looks like she might be on a dark stage caught in a spotlight. This style of lighting is known as chiaroscuro and was favoured by Italian master painter, Caravaggio. This high-contrast approach creates the impression that the light is falling on the subject from one direction, drawing her out of the gloomy background. It is an important factor in creating the drama in this print.

TRY IT YOURSELF

Prepare your paper

If you look closely, you will notice that there is a highlighted area at the front of her head which is white, while the other highlights are a softer grey colour. This effect has been achieved by creating this lighter area on the grey paper before the black is printed, perhaps by adding a diffuse circle with white spray paint.

Focus on the light

The only areas that have been carved out of the surface of the linoleum printing plate are the places where the highlights shine through. The plate has then been inked up using black ink and printed on to the grey and white of prepared paper. This is a clever way of producing a three-colour print with only one printing block.

Opposite: LaToya Hobbs, *Herero Woman*, linocut, relief ink on paper, 2015

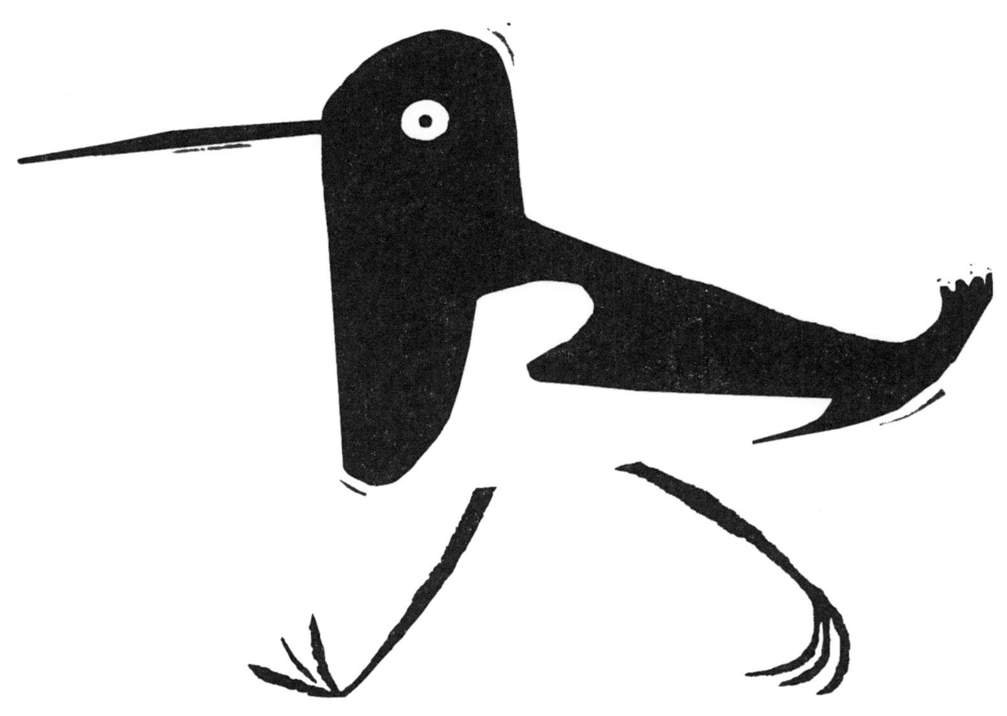

Adam Larkum, *Oyster Catcher*, lino print, oil-based ink on watercolour paper, 2007

EXPLORE THE NEGATIVE SPACE

When using one colour to print, your second colour comes from the surface you print on. So think about how you can use this creatively. What will our minds fill in when there is nothing there?

Adam Larkum uses this technique very elegantly to create the paper-white belly of his oyster catcher. His economical use of his printing plate adds a lightness of touch to this carefree bird, and engages us as the audience to fill in the missing piece. This approach suits the subject of his print as it adds to the feeling that the sun is shining so brightly in this seaside location that the oyster catcher's belly has disappeared into the glaring whitewashed wall behind him.

TRY IT YOURSELF

Refine your design
Start by sketching the design for your one-colour print, then challenge yourself to reduce it to the minimum amount of information required to communicate this design to your audience.

Consider colour combinations
Consider what the colour of paper that you will print on could bring to the design. How can you combine that with the colour of your printing ink?

EMBRACE REPETITION

Norwegian printmaker Imi Maufe has clearly been traumatized by the scourge of the Scottish summer: the midge. This tiny terror has been immortalized here in a simple but very effective way. She has created a cloud of these little insects by repeating the same small printed image many times. The carefully planned, perfectly circular 'torment of midges' has been given depth and visual interest using ghost printing.

Using only black ink, Imi Maufe has allowed the ink to run out on the printing plate rather than reapplying after each print. This is how the range of light grey to black is achieved. The single rogue midge who has escaped the swarm adds to the humour of the print. Perhaps it's just returning to the fold after a particularly satisfying meal!

TRY IT YOURSELF

Keep it simple

If you are planning a repeat print as complex as this, then it is vital to keep each individual component as simple and clear as possible.

Use silhouettes

Notice that the midge is described in silhouette with no inner detail, which evokes the sooty black appearance of the insect.

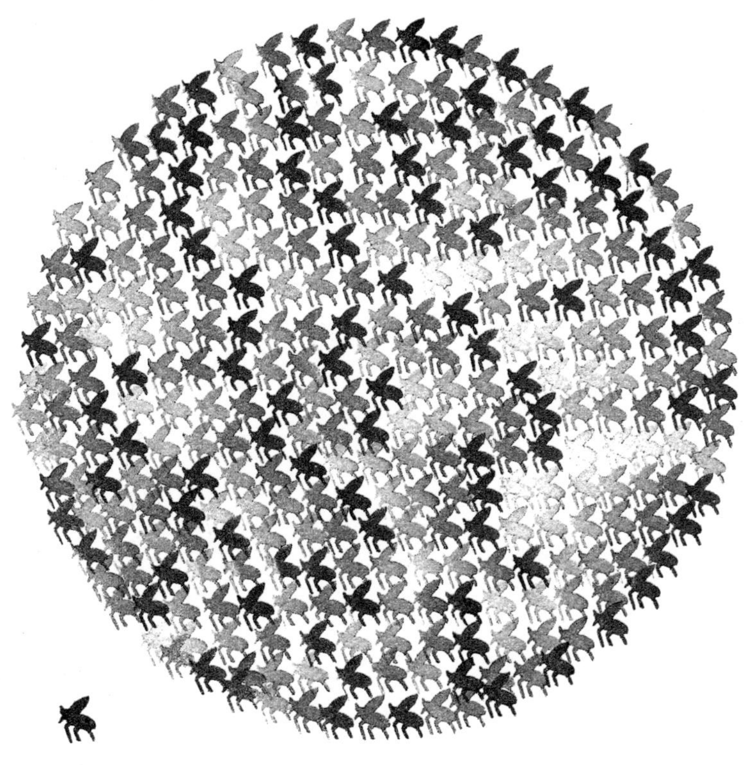

Imi Maufe, *Beware of the Midge*, rubber stamp and ink on paper, 2008

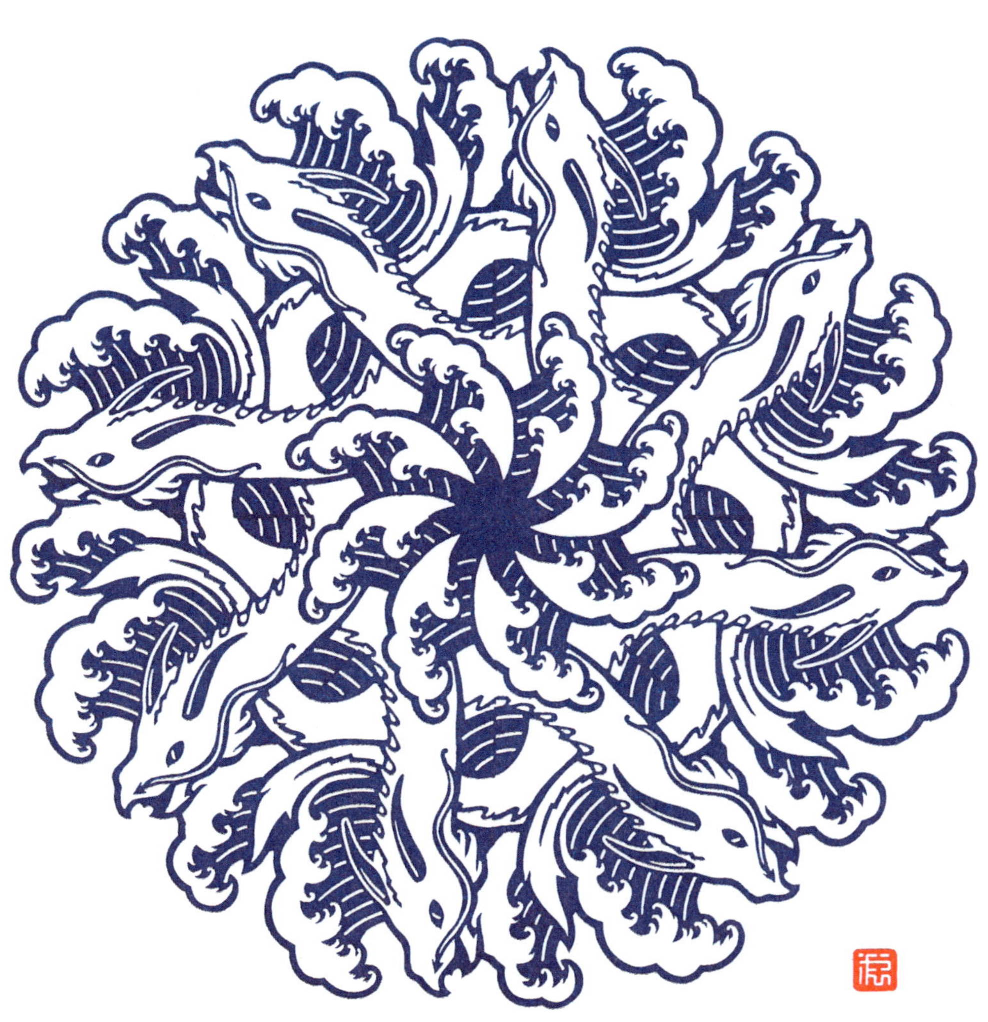

Jennifer Zee, *Make Waves*, linocut, relief ink on paper, 2021

TESSELLATION

This vortex of crashing waves and dragon heads (opposite) is a repeat print that takes the form of a wedge tessellation: a repeating pattern of interlocking shapes that fit together so perfectly that it leaves no gaps and doesn't overlap. This print is built up from a repeating pizza slice-shaped printing block that artist Jennifer Zee meticulously planned out before she started to cut it. Inspired by natural forms, traditional Japanese woodcuts and a splash of mythology, this is an elegantly complex print. The Dutch graphic artist MC Escher is also an influence, and he may be a good starting point to inspire your design when embarking on a print like this.

Praying Mantis Mandala (below) is split into 12 sections, which means each wedge is 30 degrees. When designing a tessellating print, any part of the pattern that is truncated by the shape of the printing block must continue on the opposite side of the same printing block. We will look at this in detail on the following pages.

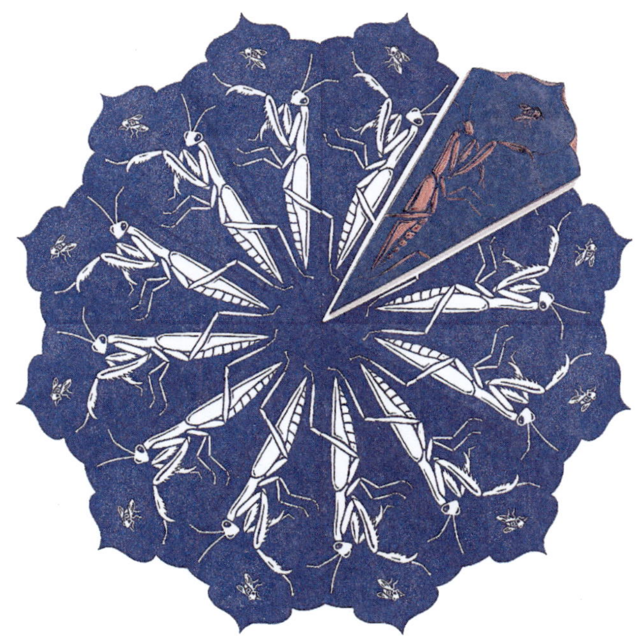

Jennifer Zee, *Praying Mantis Mandala*, linocut, relief ink on paper (block wedge included), 2021

TESSELLATION EXPLORED

When applied to printmaking, tessellation is an effective way to design a printing block that will repeat seamlessly when printed multiple times on the page. This technique was traditionally used by printed textile and wallpaper designers to create the effective interlocking patterns that decorate our homes.

Artist Brenda Holtam is a master at this technique. Her tessellating rose patch is intricate and clever. Printed onto painted paper, its bold black background creates a rambling arrangement of blooms. We can see from her design drawings how much thought and planning goes into her tessellating prints.

Opposite: Brenda Holtam, *Tudor Flowers*, lino print, relief-printing ink on painted paper, 2024

TRY IT YOURSELF

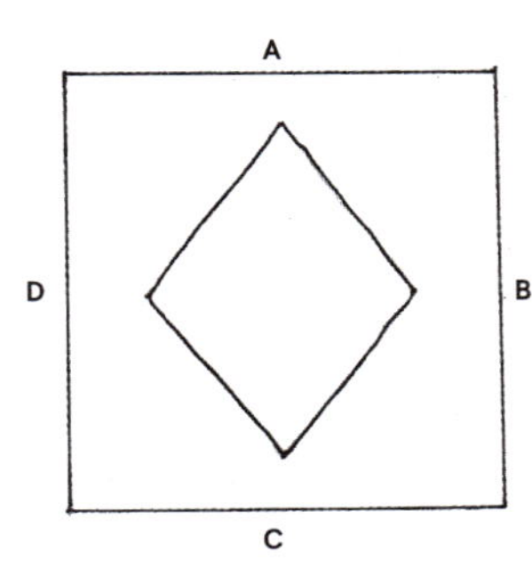

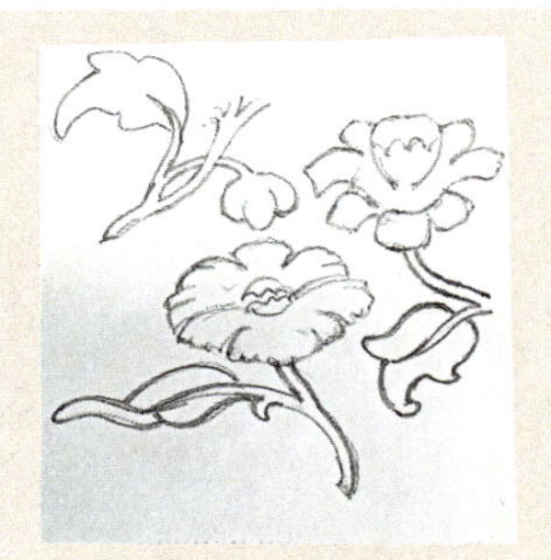

1. Cut a piece of tracing paper the exact shape of your block, which can be a square or rectangle.

2. On the tracing paper, using a soft pencil like a 2B, draw a design that does not touch the edges.

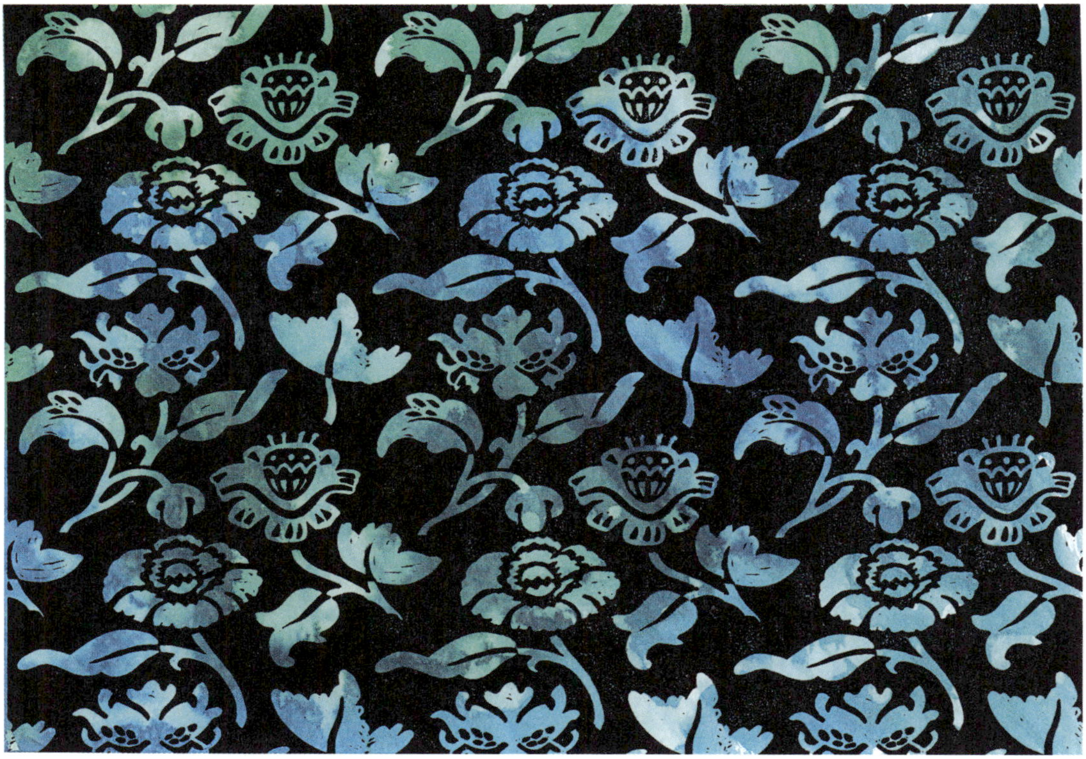

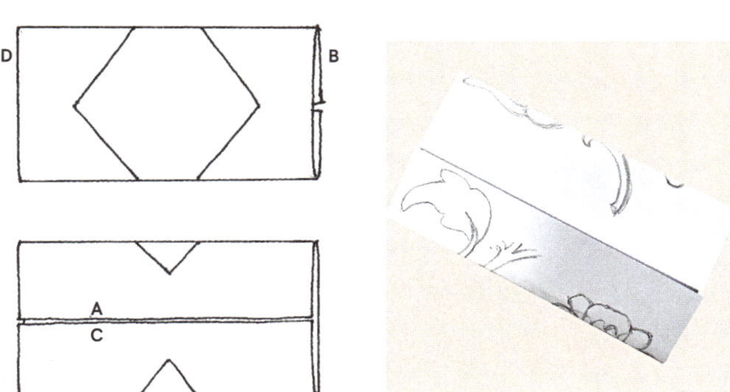

3. Fold edge A to meet edge C, with the design on the outside.

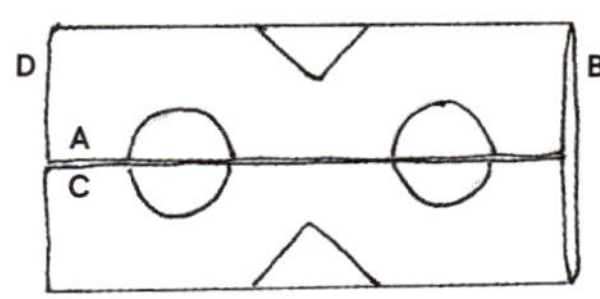

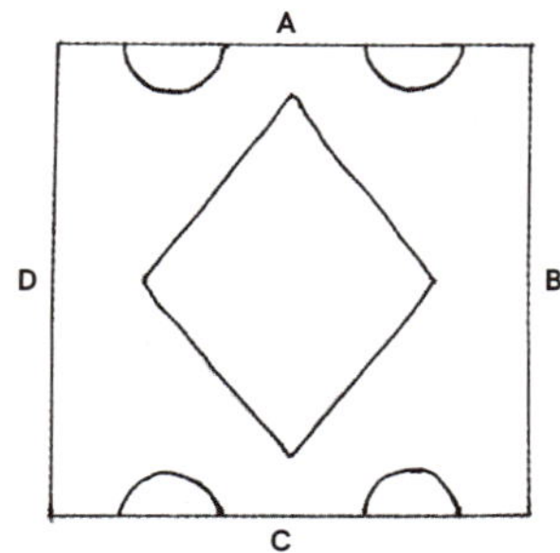

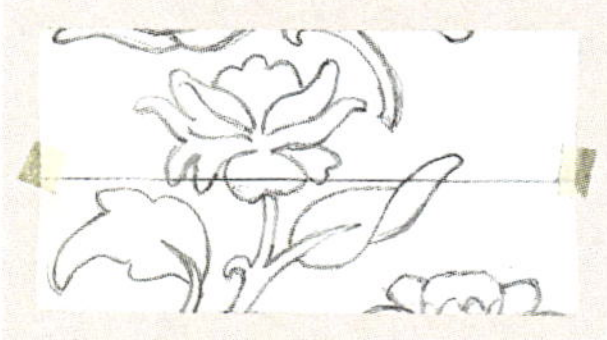

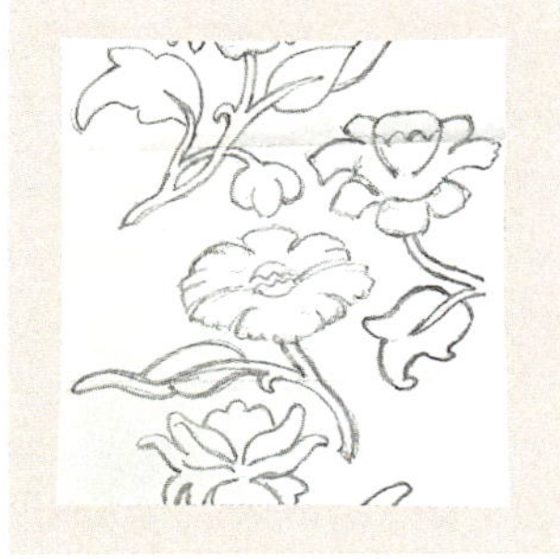

4. Continue your design drawing in the space available. Your drawing can cross the joined edges A and C, but do not let your design touch edges B and D.

5. Open the paper to see your design so far.

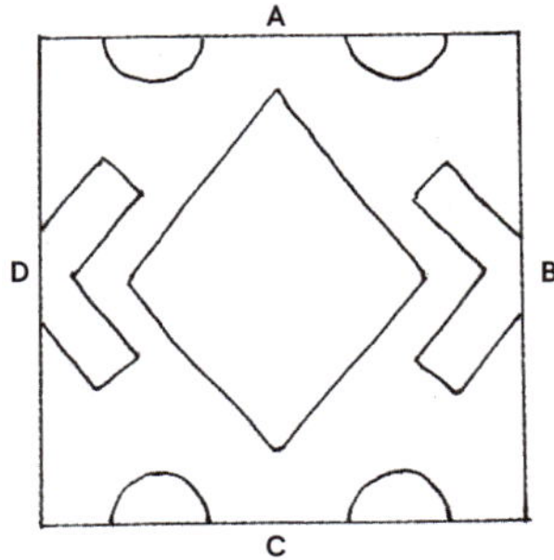

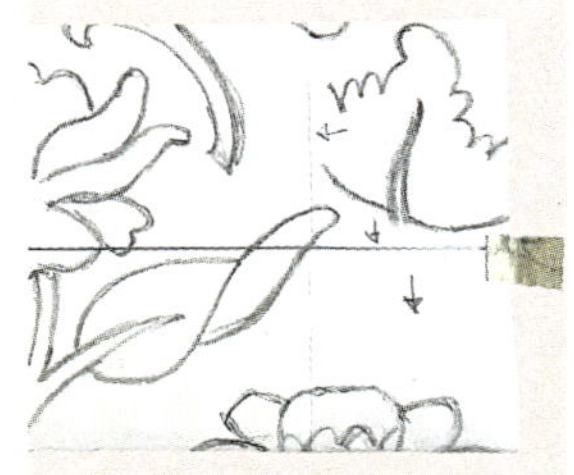

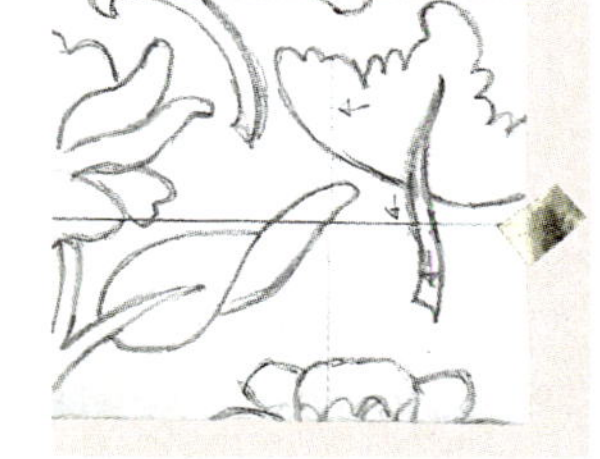

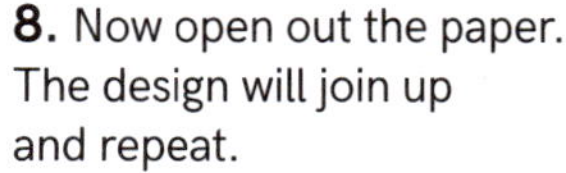

8. Now open out the paper. The design will join up and repeat.

9. Adjustments can still be made to balance the overall design. Any shape which does not touch the edges may be added or altered. If adjustments are needed for the shapes that touch the edges, the paper must be refolded while the adjustments are made.

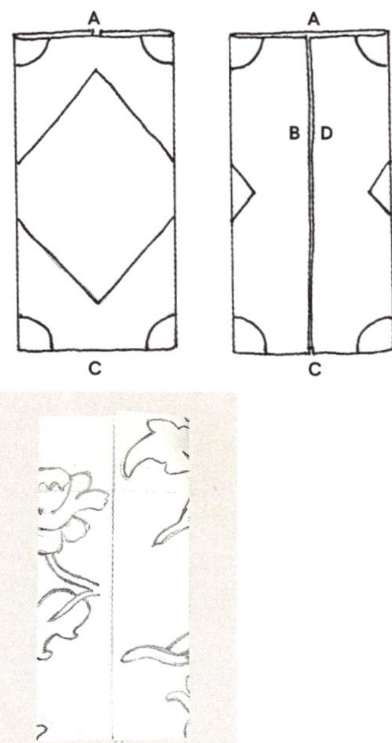

6. Now fold edge B to meet edge D. See what empty space is available to complete your design.

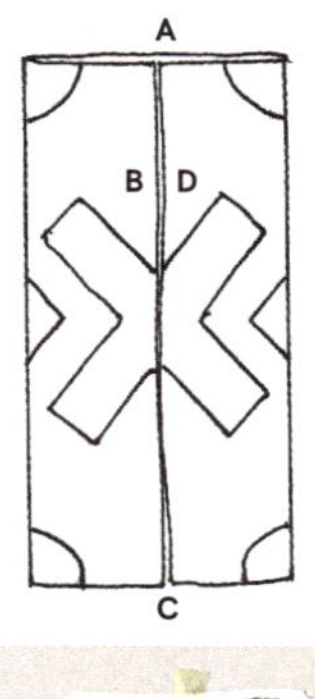

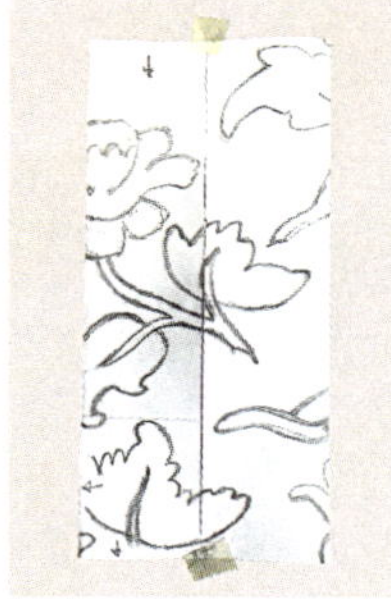

7. Again, you can draw your design across the join of edges B and D, but do not go to edges A or C.

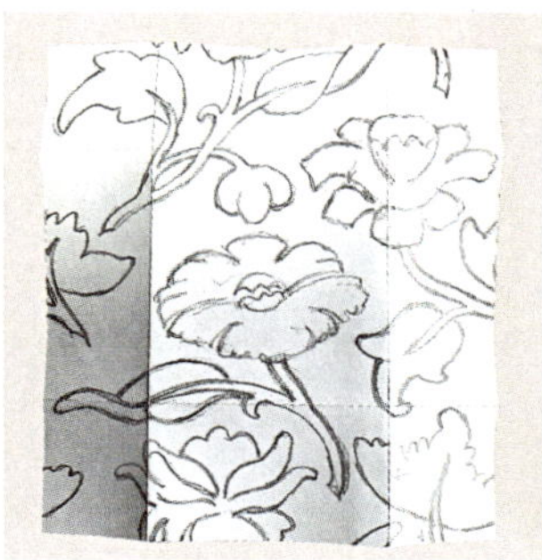

10. The design can now be transferred to your printing block. Place the paper face down onto the block and use a ballpoint pen to trace over the back of your design, applying firm pressure. This will transfer the graphite from the pencil drawing onto the surface of the block. Now you can carve the design into the block. When printing, place your block carefully so it lines up accurately.

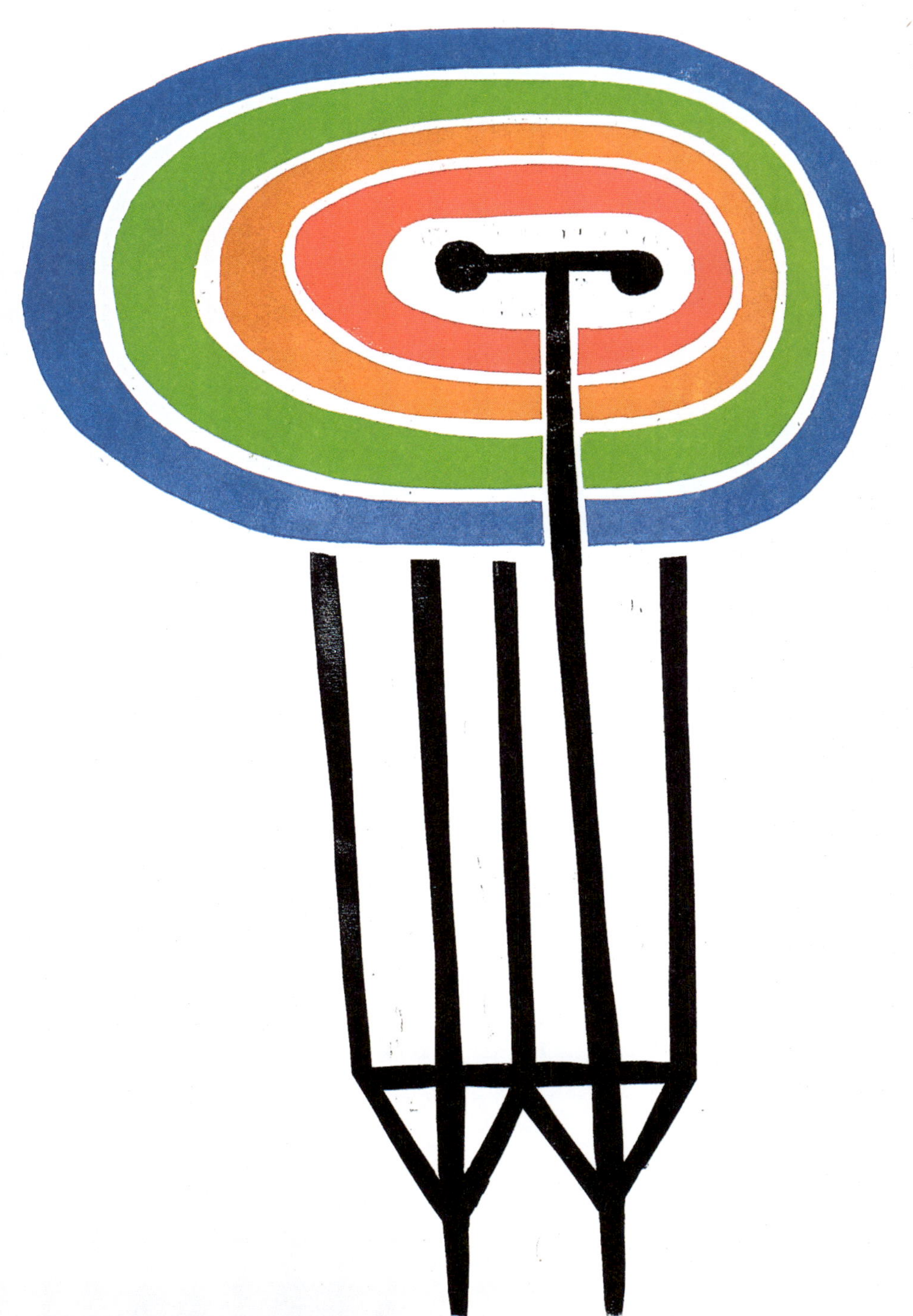

DESIGN INTERLOCKING PRINTS

One way of making a relief print which has multiple colours is by designing an interlocking printing plate that is inked up separately, then put together again like a jigsaw puzzle before printing. This means that you don't need to worry about the registration (how accurately the printing plates line up) or the colours overlapping or leaking into the wrong areas. This method works well with lino, which is easy to cut, or for a woodblock print like this one.

Drawing from his unconscious, John Pedder starts with a simple automatic drawing. By the time he has developed this dot-and-line diagram into a print design, he has built a whole character for it, which imbues the print with meaning and personality. Here, the dots become eyes on Clement's face, which gives him a rather withering look, suggesting that he is a little annoyed as he gazes off into the distance. This print works so well because it tunes into our natural tendency to see faces in objects.

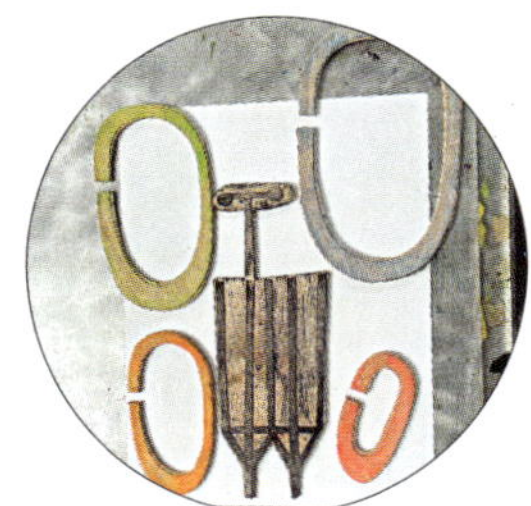

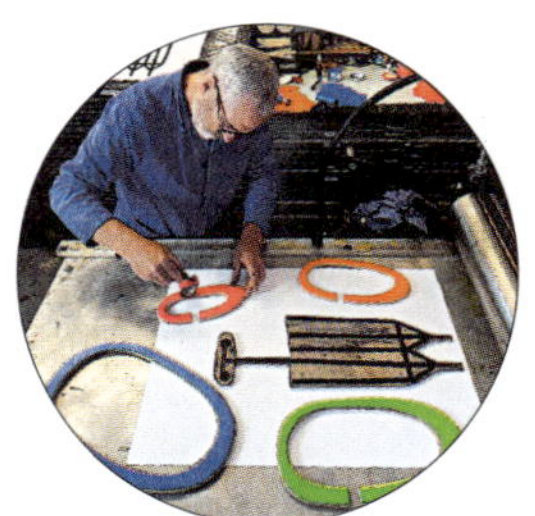

TRY IT YOURSELF

1. Start by planning out your print with your colours in mind. You don't want to end up with too many small jigsaw pieces, so work big and bold.

2. Draw the reversed image onto the printing block as usual.

3. Now you can cut your printing plate into the planned colour sections. If working on lino, it is better to do this before you carve the design as it will be stronger, so easier to handle and cut.

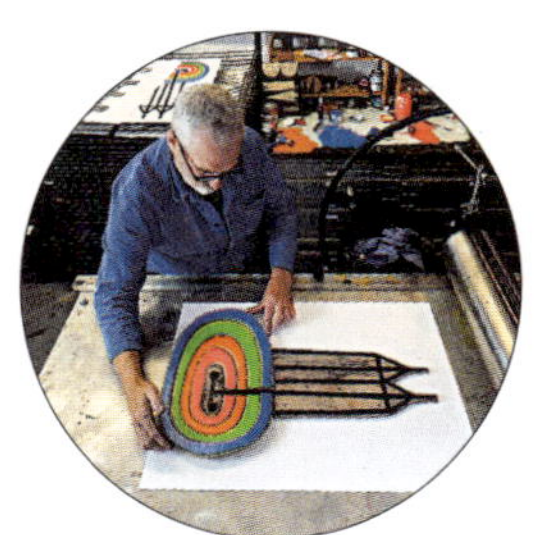

4. Using a discarded piece, practise cutting the printing-block material first so that you are confident with controlling the blade. If you are using lino, you will be able to cut your block using a sharp craft knife. If you are working on wood, a hacksaw with a sharp, new blade will be most effective.

5. Now you can carefully carve out your design.

6. When printing, you can ink up each section separately before carefully fitting them back together, then taking your print.

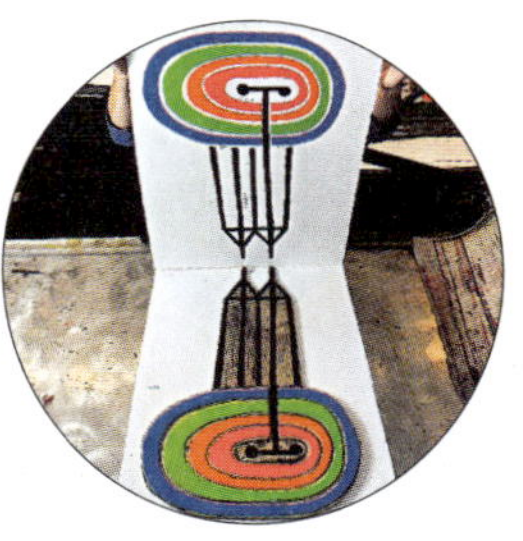

Opposite: John Pedder, *Clement*, woodcut print, relief ink on paper, 2024

TWO-COLOUR PRINT

Another way to make a multicolour print is by using two printing blocks the same size and shape to print different colours over each other, thereby creating a two-colour print. This is what Adam Larkum has done here. The light-blue block is treated rather like a wash of colour, carved to look like brush marks, which gives it a lightness of touch. His colour choice of a light translucent blue is reminiscent of a watercolour wash, which adds to this effect. These freer marks contrast nicely with the other block which provides the solid outline and bold dark-blue marks of the shading lines. They combine to give his bowler-hatted chap a looseness that is unusual to see in lino prints.

To align the two blocks of his print accurately, Adam's method is to carve the first block with the detailed outline of his character. Then he makes a print of that using dark ink onto some cheap photocopier paper. While that print is still sticky, he presses it onto his second block, making sure it lines up with his first print. This leaves a reversed print of the character on the second block as a reference image for where to put his second colour. Now he can draw the second colour design on this piece of lino and carve that.

TRY IT YOURSELF

1. Make sure the two blocks are the same size and shape as this will affect how they line up, or register, when you come to print them.

2. When you make the first print onto the cheap photocopier paper, make pencil marks where the four corners of the printing block lie.

3. When you transfer the design onto the second block make sure you line up that block's four corners with your pencil marks so that the image will be in the same place on the second block.

4. When you come to print your image, experiment with the order in which you print the colours and see how this affects the final image.

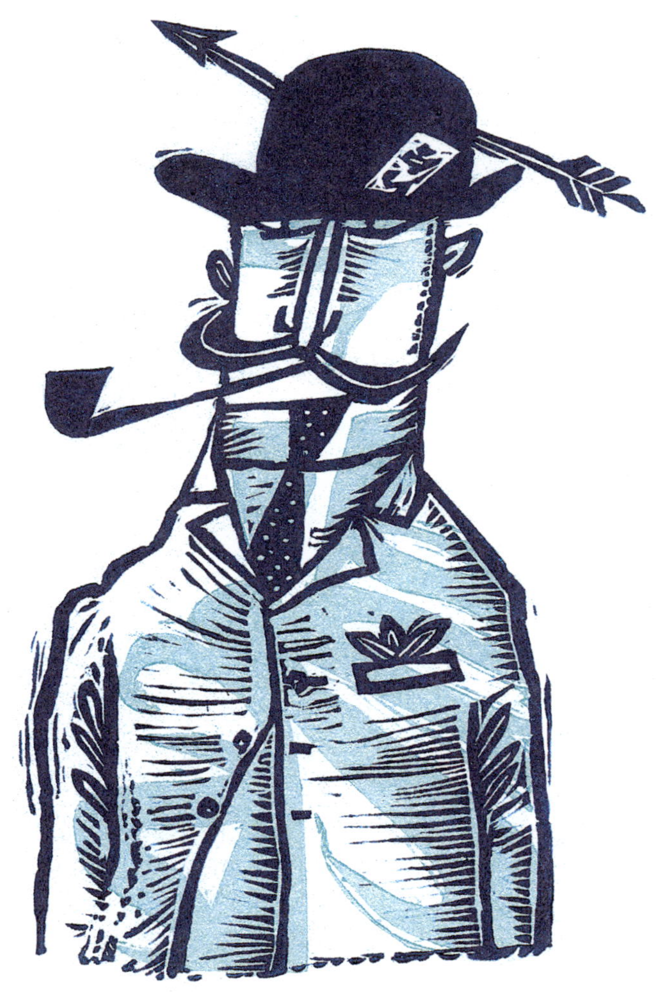

Adam Larkum, *Man in Bowler Hat*, lino print, oil-based ink on watercolour paper, 2010

TWO-COLOUR PRINT EXPLORED

This print is made in two passes using two printing plates that are the same size. The first fills in the body colour and the second provides the black outlines.

TRY IT YOURSELF

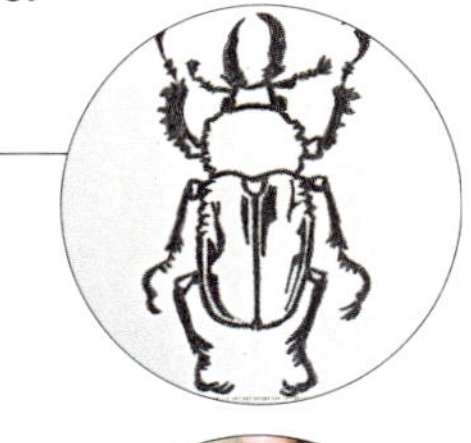

1. When you are creating a design drawing for a linocut, it's all about simplifying. Here, the solid colour of the body of the beetle is set off by the bold, black outlines.

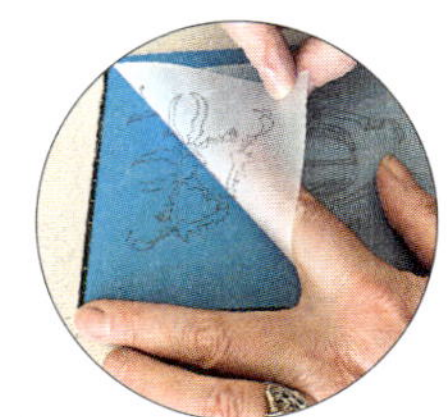

2. Once you are happy with your sketch, copy it onto a sheet of tracing paper which is larger than the two printing plates you will be using.

3. Transfer your drawing to the first plate by tracing it onto the paper, flipping the paper over and rubbing the back so the graphite lifts onto the surface of the plate and the image is reversed. This is important as it will be reversed again when printed, making it the right way round.

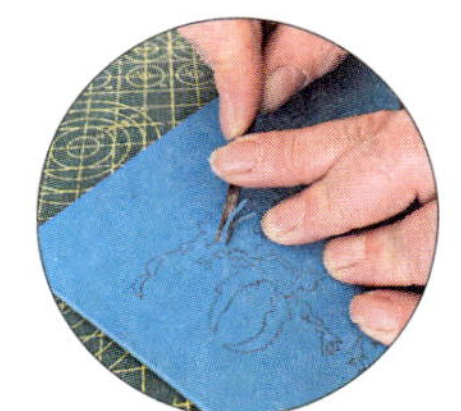

4. To make sure the drawing is in the same position on both plates, mark the four corners of the plate onto the tracing paper. You can line these marks up when you repeat this process to transfer the drawing onto the second plate.

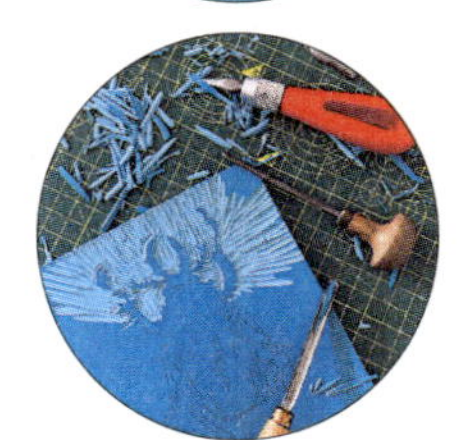

5. Now you can start carving. There are two basic shapes of linocutting blade. The V-shape blades are for edges and the U-shaped blades are for clearing large areas. Start by carefully following the edges of your design using a V-shaped blade.

6. When clearing out the lino with a U-shaped blade, think about which direction you want to cut in, as you might want a trace of these lines in your final design. In this example, the flowing lines add a dynamism to the print.

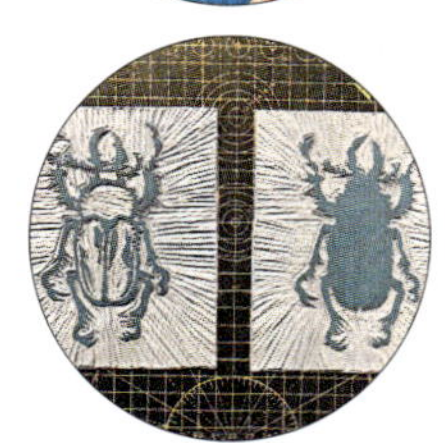

7. When clearing large areas, make sure that you follow two basic rules: always keep your non-dominant hand behind the direction of the cut to avoid injury; and always clear away from the main 'body' of your design to limit the potential damage to your plate if your hand slips.

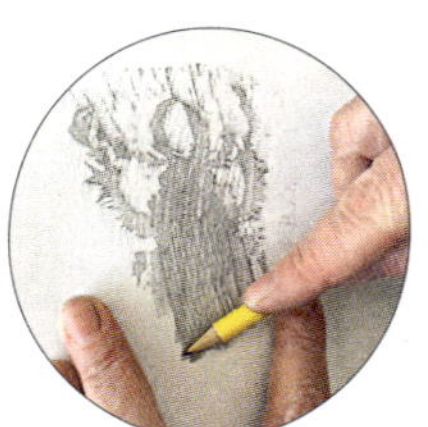

8. To check your cut before you get your inks out, use the side of a graphite pencil to take a rubbing of the plate on a scrap piece of paper.

9. Next, draw around the outline of your plates on a thick piece of cardboard and cut it out to make a frame to hold your printing plates. This will help you to register them so that they line up when printing.

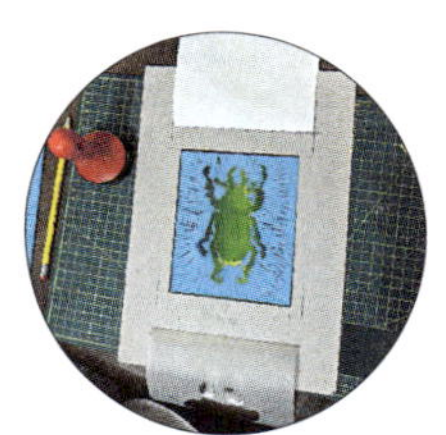

10. To create a mask to control the transfer of ink onto the paper, cut the drawing out of tracing paper. You can see it here. It is flipped up onto the plate after it has been inked and before it is printed.

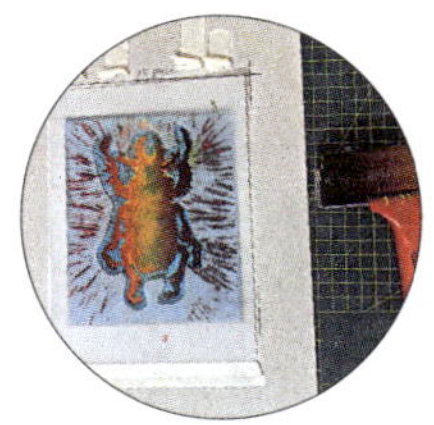

11. Roll out two colours of ink in parallel, then ink up the solid fill plate. Place your plate in the frame, position the paper, then mark the edge of the first piece of printing paper where it sits on the cardboard frame with a pencil. Attach tape to hold each subsequent piece of paper in the same position to register the prints. Print a series of beetle 'bodies' by applying pressure to the back of the paper using your hand or a baren.

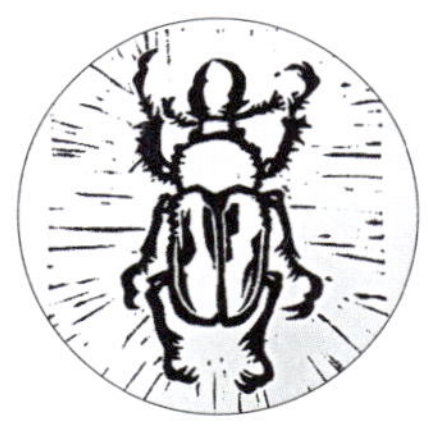

12. Make a test print of the black outline plate, then reattach the dry 'body' prints in the same position and repeat the printing process with the outline plate inked up with black to complete the print. If you don't want the dynamic lines, simply reuse the tracing-paper mask.

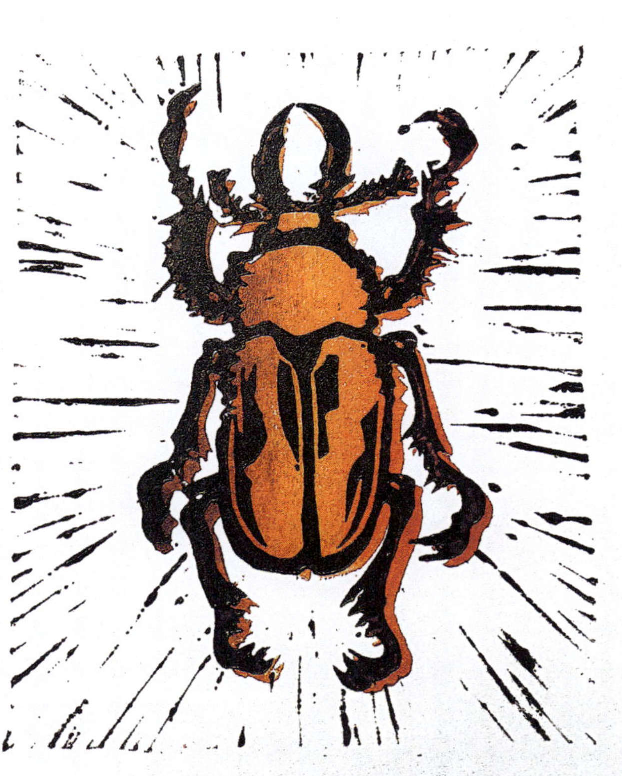

Eve Blackwood, *Rainbow Stag Beetle*, linocut, relief ink on paper, 2024

MULTI-COLOUR LINO PRINT

This complex print was achieved in five passes through the printing press and its success lies in two areas: careful registration and great planning. Let's look closely at this lino print by Marjorie Accarier to really appreciate the level of planning that went into it.

Each separate printing colour had its own carved printing block. Those colours are: gold, bronze, teal, light blue, then the bronze again. The artist cleverly planned the print to maximize the effect of these colours and minimize the need for outlines.

Look carefully: the characters' edges are defined by the difference in colour between them and the character, or the background, behind.

- The first colour is the gold background. The only areas not printed are the ten small eye shapes which are left the original colour of the paper: white.

- Then comes the second pass with the bronze, which covers all the print apart from the white eyes, and describes the wild hair and outline of the largest figure.

- The mid tone is next. Teal overprints the large figure in two places: defining the second largest figure and giving us the outline of the smallest figure, but leaving the object they are holding bronze. This colour is also allowed to print circles over the white of the eyes which provides their irises.

- Next comes the lighter blue colour which fills in all the faces and surrounds the held object. This allows the artist to describe the shape of the smallest character's fingers.

- Finally comes the fifth pass with the bronze colour which outlines all the characters' features and the pupils in their eyes. This gives the print definition and the characters' personality. Their eyes lead us around the composition as they dart about in different directions.

Opposite: Marjorie Accarier, *The Guides*, lino print, ink on Olin paper, 2023

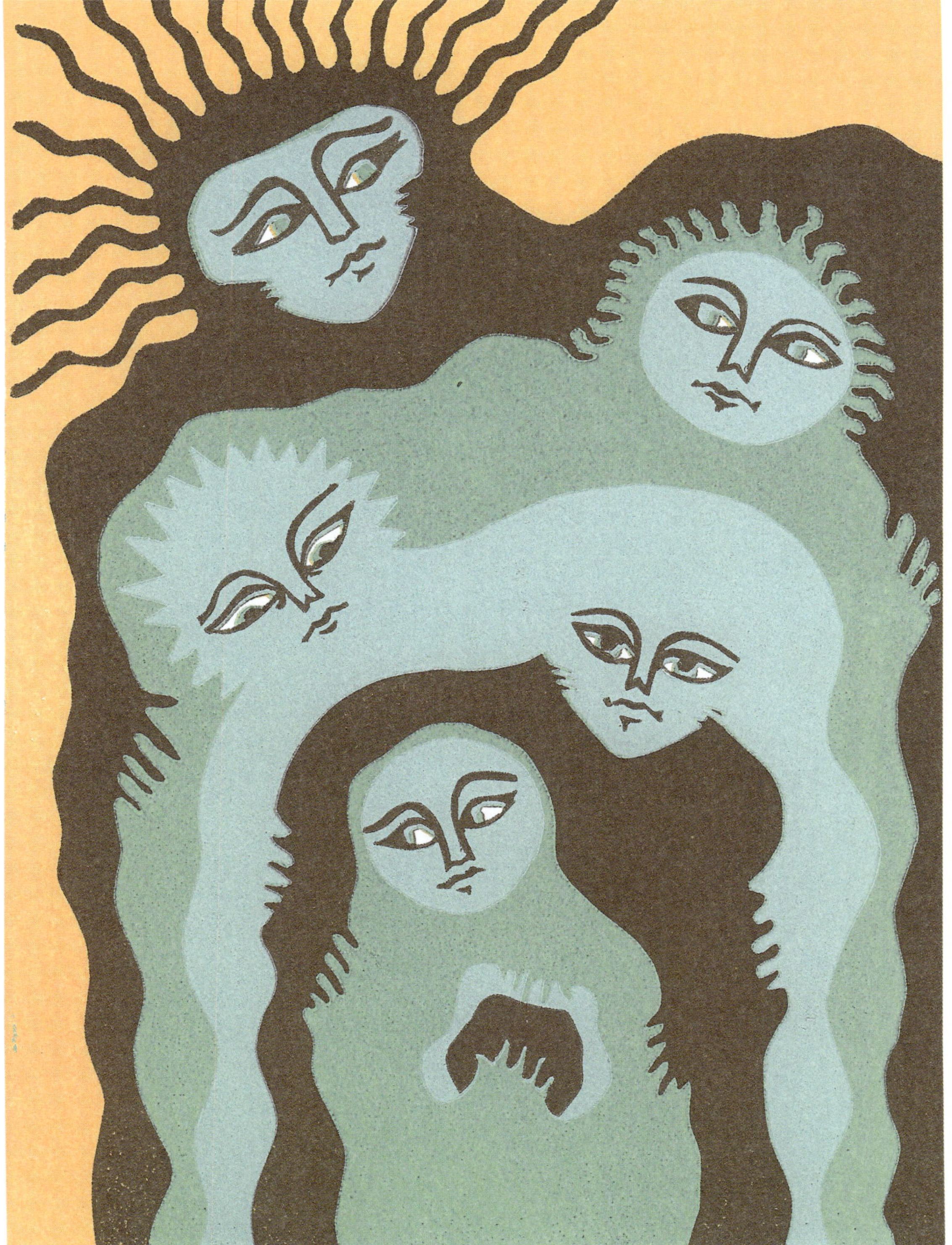

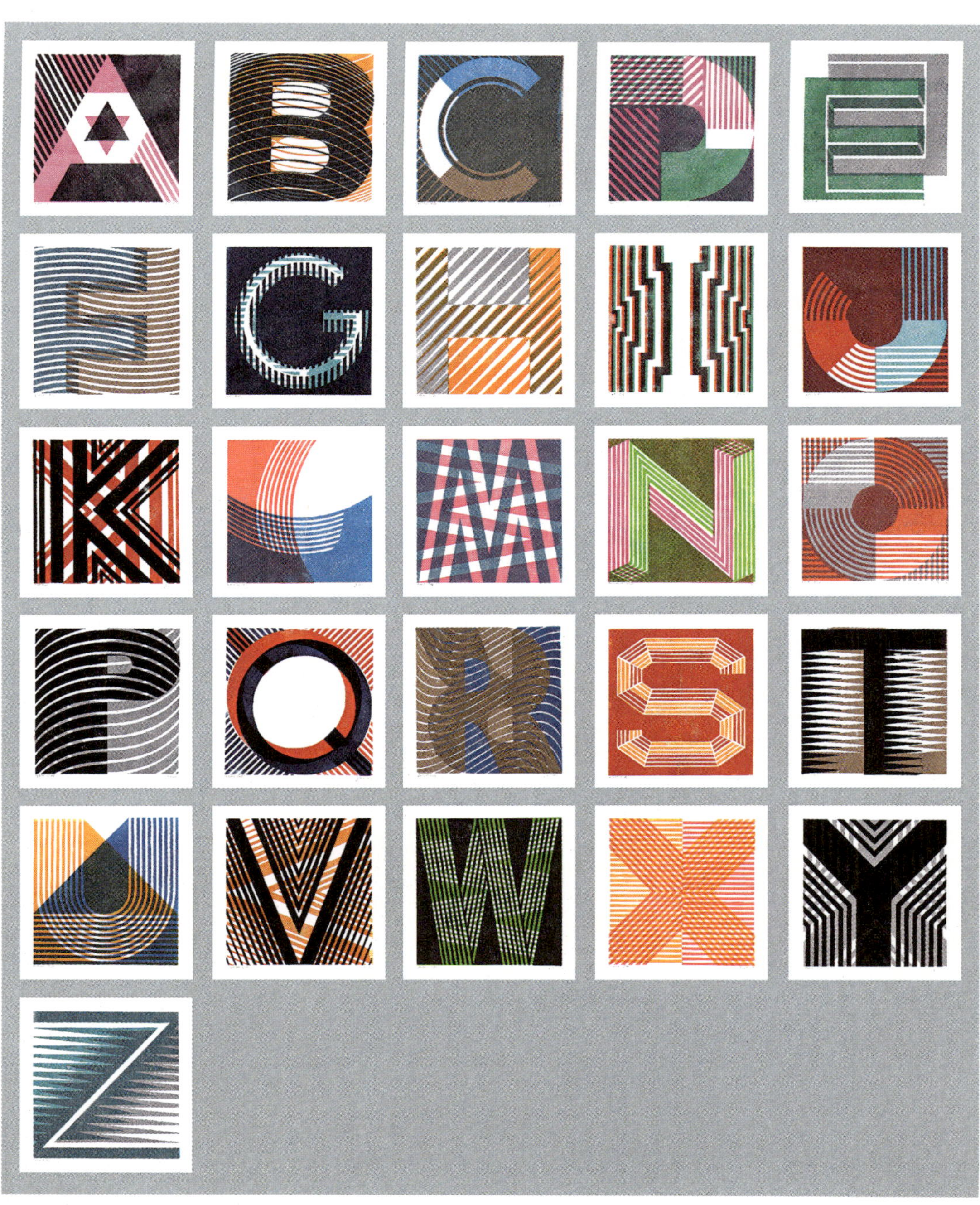

James Brown, *A-Z lino-cut prints*, relief-printing ink on paper, 2013

CREATE VISUAL ENERGY BY OVERPRINTING

This is so clever! Once you've worked out how these prints are produced, you'll feel like you've figured out an elegant puzzle. Designer James Brown has brilliantly worked out how to create the letters of the alphabet by printing the same block twice in different colours. By rotating these simple cuts by either 90 or 180 degrees, he creates energetic and clever optical effects that reveal each letter. The design of the blocks is important. He designs them to have flat areas of colour, white areas that let the colours shine through and more complicated areas of precisely cut lines that create rhythmic composite patterns when overprinted. His colour choices are key: he chooses analogous colours like the orange and red of the S which create harmony; or complementary colours like the orange and blue of the U which create visual energy; or two colours like the red and cyan of the J designed to mix and create the third maroon colour that gives the letter its outline.

TRY IT YOURSELF

Patterns

By placing the Y carefully in the centre of the block, it retains balance and predictability in an otherwise visually complex image. The precise repeating outlines intersect to create a complex pattern around the letter, sending waves of energy across the page.

Placement

Purposefully not placing the Q in the dead centre of its block allows space for the all-important tail of the Q which sets it apart from an O.

Flow

The patterns used reflect the characteristics of the letters themselves. For example, the P has a lovely curving elegance, while the Z has a zigzagging pointiness.

SIMPLE COLOUR MIXING

One of the most important things to understand when designing a multicolour print is how simple colours can be mixed to create new colours. Here is an easy way to get your head round how that works.

TRY IT YOURSELF

1. Start by making a simple design on your piece of lino. The image can be anything you like, but make sure it has some negative space (areas where no ink will print), some solid blocks of colour and an area which has hatching (parallel lines that create a halftone effect).

2. The primary colours (red, yellow and blue) are the base of every other colour, so they are a good place to start your colour-mixing journey. First, make a series of prints in blue ink, then do the same in yellow and then red so that you have at least three prints of each starting colour.

3. Once these prints are dry, ink up your printing block again using one of the other coloured inks, and then print over the original colour to layer this colour on top.

4. Depending on the order in which you combine these colours, you will achieve different effects. This is because some colours are naturally more dominant than others. Due to the amount of pigment in the ink, yellow is usually the most translucent colour, then red and lastly blue, which is the most dominant.

5. You can alter this mixing balance by introducing ghost printing to the process. If you use the second or third printing of the block without re-inking it, you will create prints which are less saturated and therefore more translucent, allowing the colours to mix more effectively.

6. Rotating the printing block each time you print it will also allow you to see the mixing process more clearly. It is worth noting the colours' order and strength on these prints, so that you will always have a reference for colour mixing when you come to design your next multicolour print.

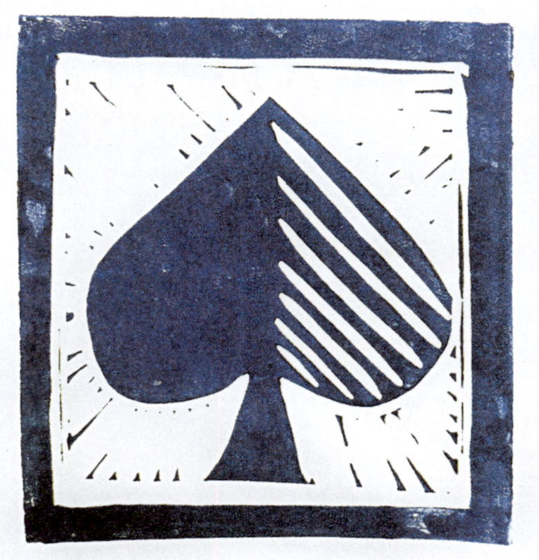
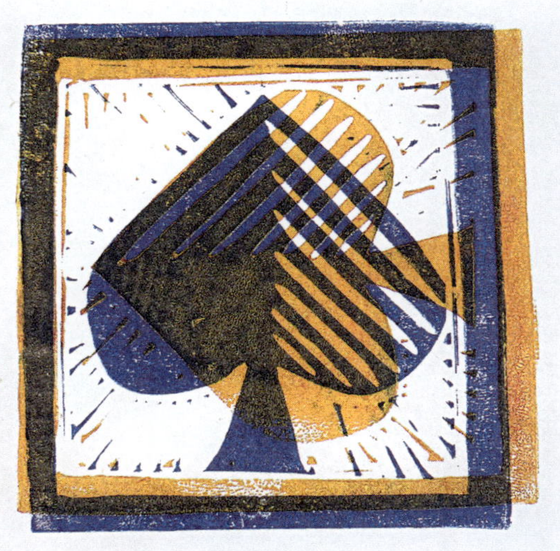
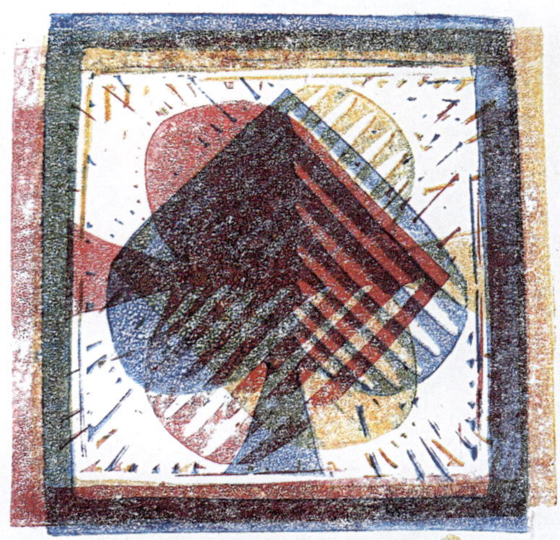
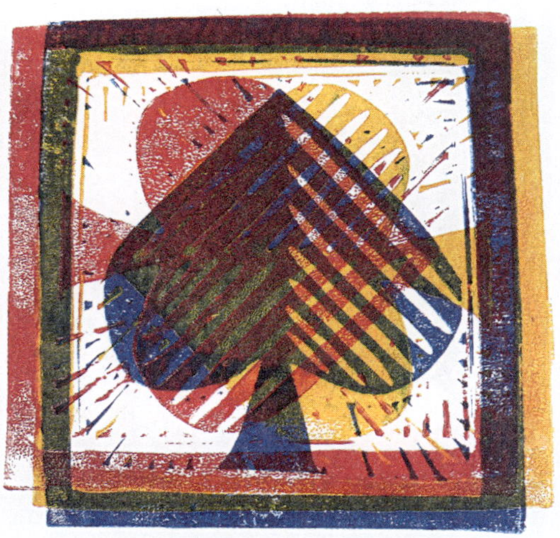

Eve Blackwood, *Ace of Spades*, lino print, relief ink on paper, 2024

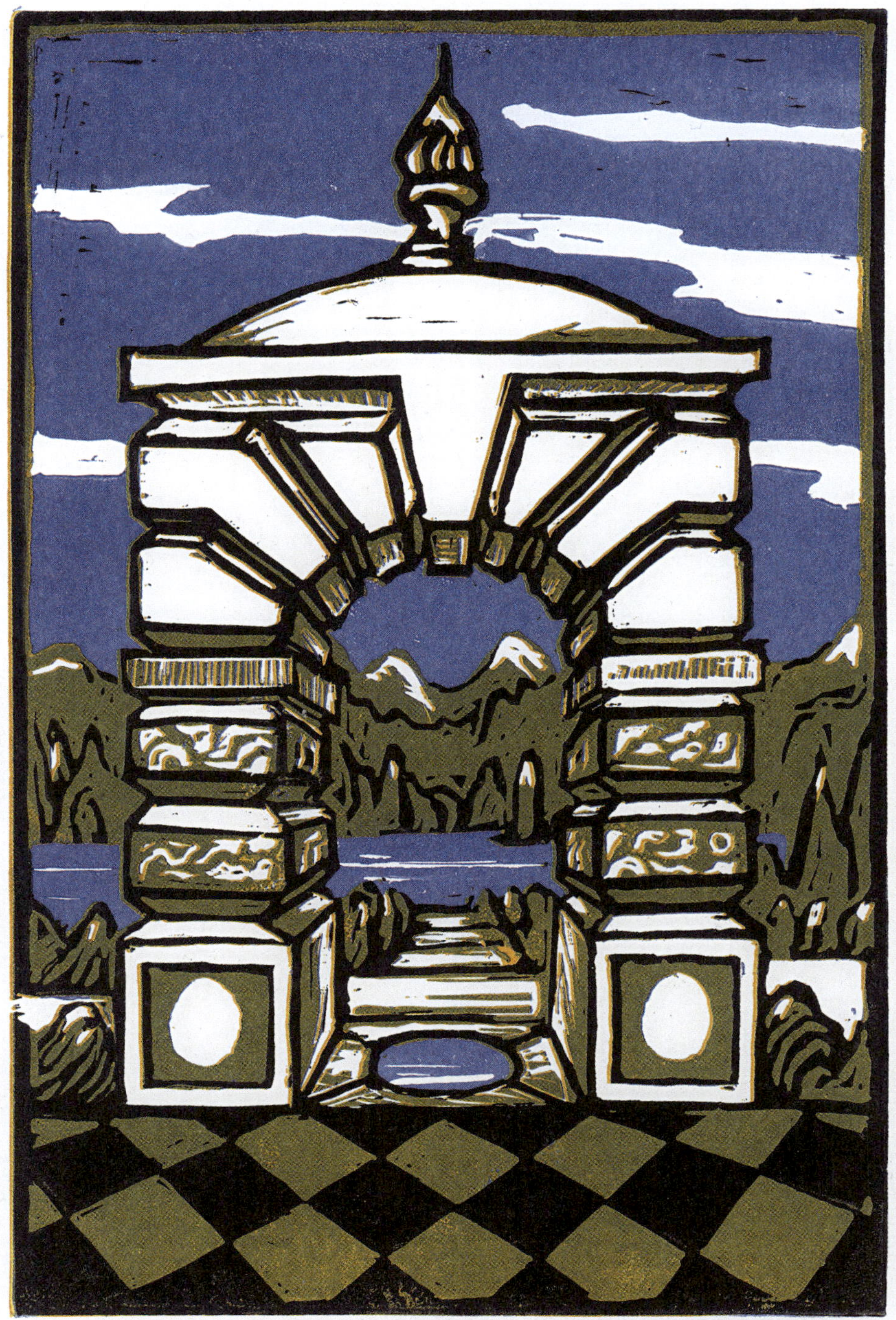

REDUCTION LINO PRINTING

Opposite: Howard Vie, *Wellhead*, lino print, lino-printing ink on watercolour paper, 2024

The reduction method uses only one printing block which is altered after every colour is printed. The limitation of this method is that you can only ever have as many prints as you make using the first colour, as it will not be possible to reprint that stage once you have altered the block.

TRY IT YOURSELF

1. Start with the one colour which is in its original, unmixed form in your print design. In Howard Vie's print the colour is blue. This colour then forms the basis of every colour mix that you subsequently create by printing on top of it, so before you start you need to plan how those colours will mix. At this point, your printing block will look very simple, with only the areas you want to keep white removed. Make more of these prints than you think you will need to leave room for error.

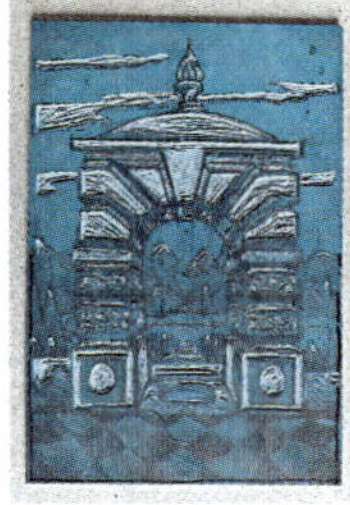

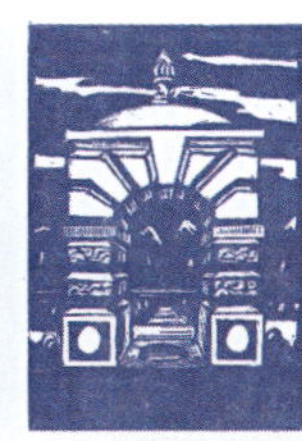

2. Now you can alter your printing block before printing the next colour. Here, the second colour is yellow, so Howard has carved away the areas on the block where he wants to preserve the blue and left the rest. He carefully lines up the block so that it is in the same place as it was for the first print. This means that the colours will align, or register, perfectly. He now has a white, blue and green print because the blue and yellow have mixed to make green.

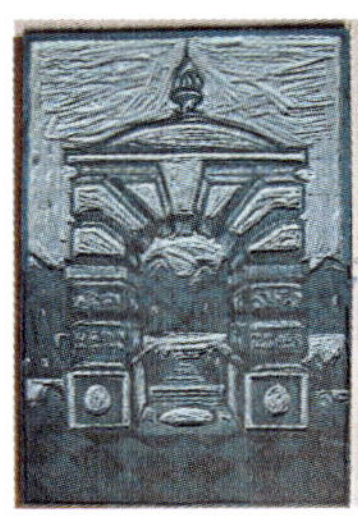

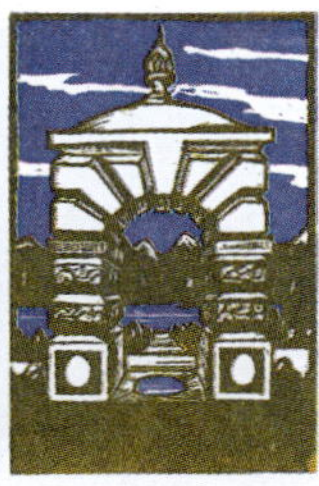

3. In this example, the last colour is black, so Howard once again alters his original block, carving away the areas where he wants to preserve the green. This leaves only the black tiles and outlines, which add definition to the image.

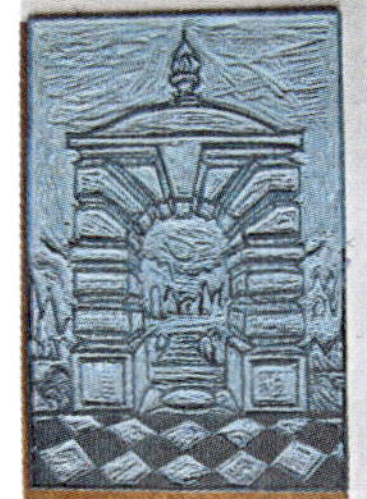

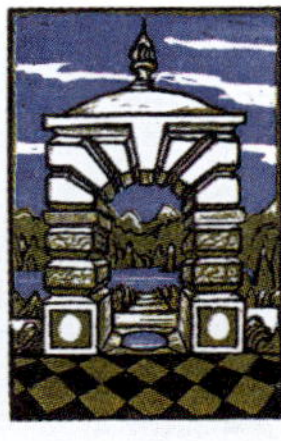

4. Now the print is complete. Depending on how well the colours have been printed and how precise his registration is, Howard will have a maximum edition of the number of blue prints he made at the beginning. He will not be able to create a second edition, or experiment with different colour combinations, as he would be able to with a multi-block print.

EXPERIMENT WITH EMBOSSING

One of the great advantages of using a printing press is the embossing effect that we can see in Matt Roussel's *Scarabe* print. He is using the negative space around the beetle to add interest by controlling the gouges he makes with the cutting tool so they form concentric shapes. These shapes ripple out from the beetle like the surface of water. The outer shape of the printing block now matters because this contains these marks. Here, Matt chose a lozenge shape reminiscent of an Egyptian cartouche, which fits rather beautifully with the motif of the scarab beetle.

Embossing is particularly effective when you use a dampened heavyweight paper like this to print on, as the indenting will be much more pronounced and will contrast with the natural textured surface of the paper. If you are applying the ink on the same pressing, you will have to be careful not to make the paper too damp as it will make the ink bleed and you will not achieve the wonderful crisp edges to the colour that we see here. The black ink of the beetle sinks into the indents created by the beetle's body, increasing the impression of relief in the print and creating the illusion of it as a carved, lacquered object.

TRY IT YOURSELF

Two passes

You might like to make this style of print in two passes. The first, from an uninked plate, would give you the embossing effect. Then, once the paper is fully dry, you can carefully line up the embossed paper to the inked plate for a second pass. This will fill in the areas you want to be coloured, giving you precise edges to the colour with no bleeding.

Use a stencil

You could place a hand-cut paper stencil over the block when you roll on the ink. This will limit the inked area, keeping the embossed area clean.

Dampen the paper

The carved lines are picked up by dampening the paper before printing with it. This softens the fibres in the paper, which allows it to be moulded into these incised areas when it is put under pressure by the rollers of a printing press.

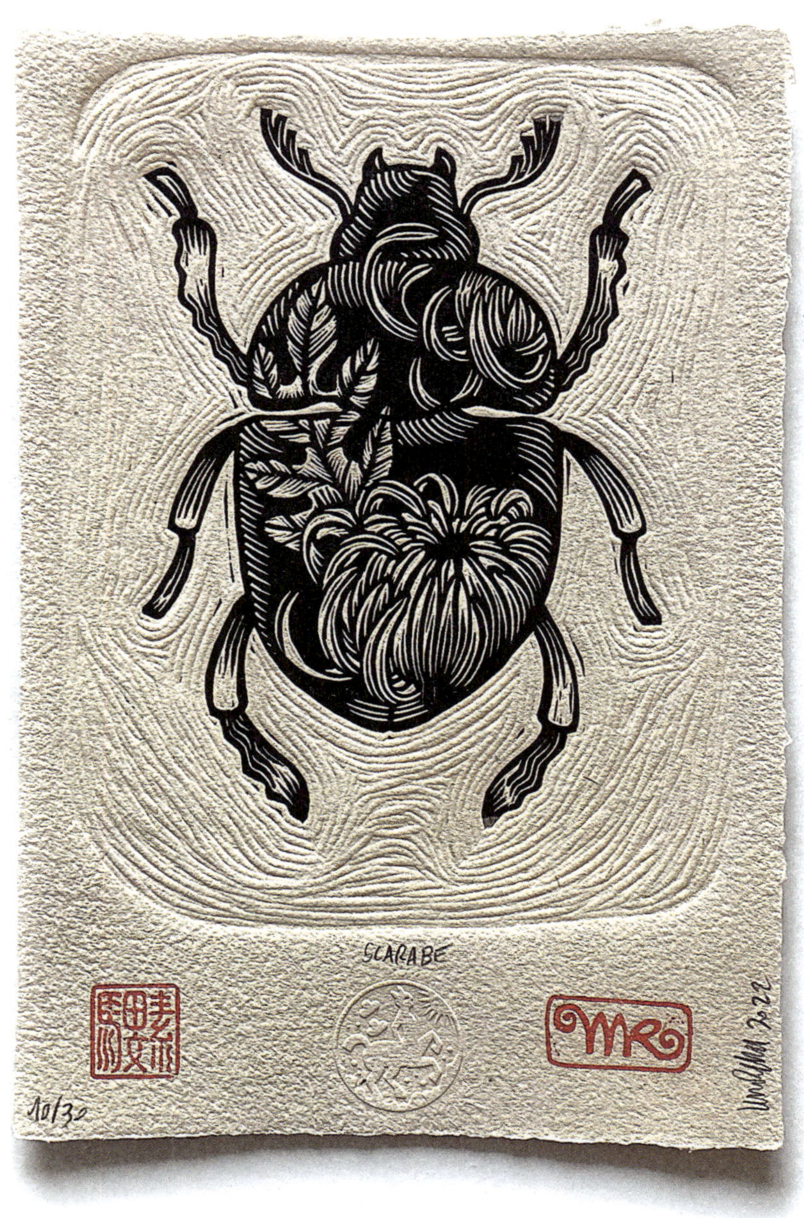

Matt Roussel, *Scarabe*, woodcut print, aquawash ink on handmade paper, 2022

INTAGLIO PRINTING

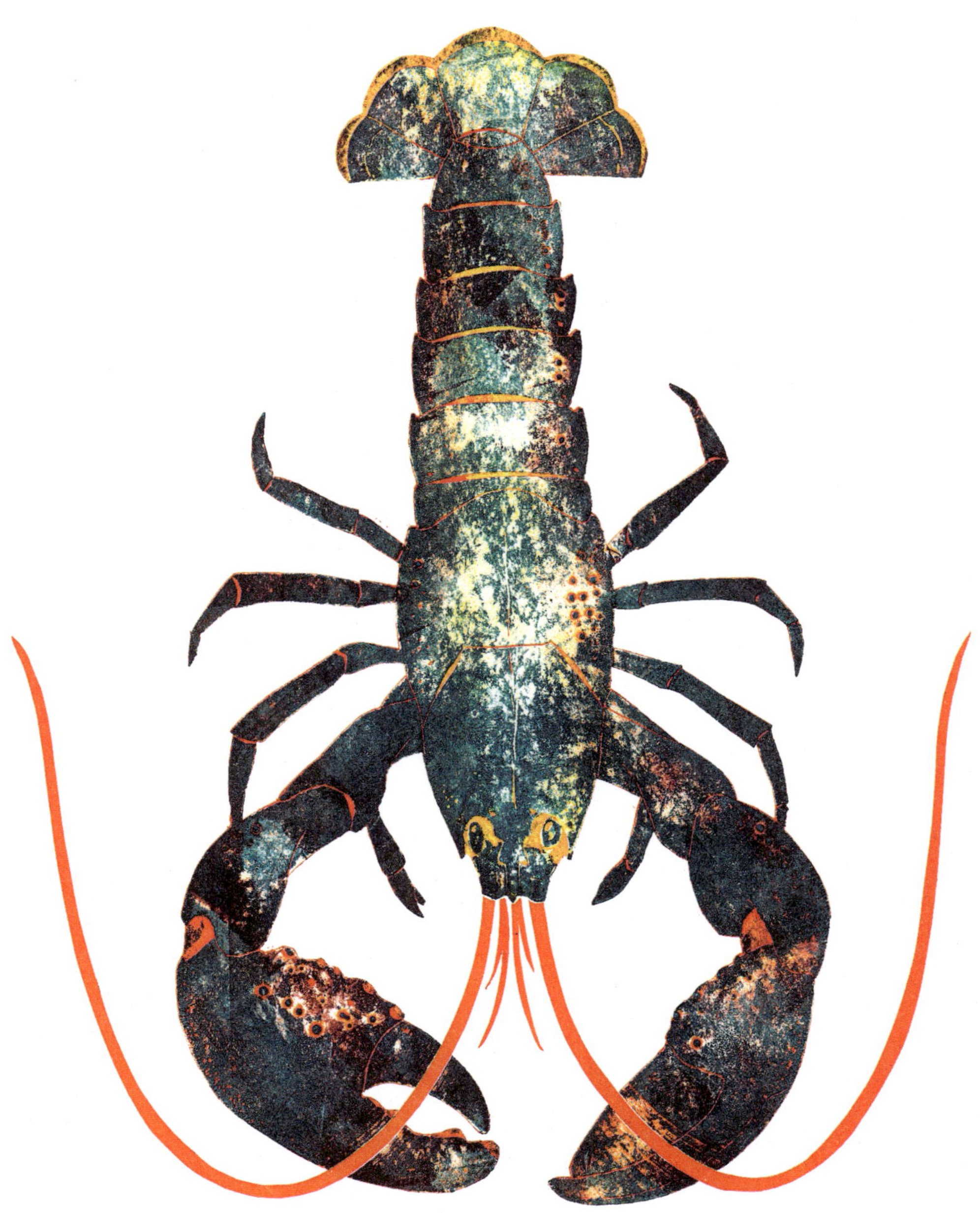

Steph Renshaw, *Lobster*, intaglio print made using collagraph and drypoint on acid-free etching paper, 2019

SCRATCH THE SURFACE

Steph Renshaw has used a medium-weight card with a water-resistant plastic film coating on it for the printing plate of this collagraph. She has created some fabulously complex colours by mixing and rubbing back the silky intaglio inks she has applied, allowing the surface of the card to bring texture to the lobster's shell. Adding incised lines and raised dots to the claws and body, she has rubbed back or allowed the ink to gather to create little barnacles of colour. By inking the antennae separately, from a complementary orangey-red to the greeny-blue of the shell, she injects a lovely energy to the print.

In this section of the book, we will be looking at artists who use intaglio printing. This covers any form of printing where a printing surface has been scratched to create the image. Intaglio comes from the Italian word 'intagliare' which means 'incise'. Etching and drypoint are both types of intaglio print and we will look at them later in this chapter. However, intaglio is sometimes incorporated into collagraphs and this lobster print is an example of that. All these intaglio techniques work best when using a printing press because you need pressure to force the dampened printing paper into the incised lines on the plate.

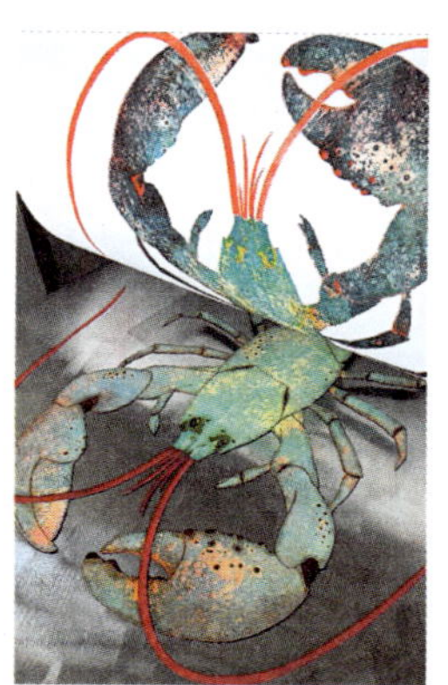

TRY IT YOURSELF

Inking up

Once the plate is ready to print, the ink is applied. A rag, and then pieces of stiff tissue paper, are used to rub the ink off the surface, leaving it in the incised scratches to create sharp lines, and in the places where the artist wants to create areas of tone or colour.

Dampen your paper

The printing paper is dampened to make it soft enough to sink into the scratches and pick up the ink when it is put through the rollers of the press. This also embosses the print, leaving the impression of the edges of the plate and any raised areas of texture on the printing surface.

Accessing a printing press

You can access a printing press by joining a print workshop. Alternatively, there are also lightweight, small, easy-to-use and affordable printing presses available to buy if you have the space and budget for one at home. Using a press will allow you to expand your printmaking horizons.

COLLAGE YOUR PRINTING PLATE

This fascinatingly intricate print of a dilapidated building is made from the simplest materials. The basic printing plate is a piece of cardboard that has been modified to produce a wide range of textures and marks that will hold or repel the ink in different ways. Emma Willemse has cut and collaged to transform this card into a collagraph plate. The dense dark shadows are areas where the smooth surface of cardboard has been removed to reveal the more absorbent material below. When printed, this will create an area of textured tone that is reminiscent of the rough ground at the building site. She has added pieces of card and string to create distinct lines, and patches of hessian to create blocks of cross-hatched texture.

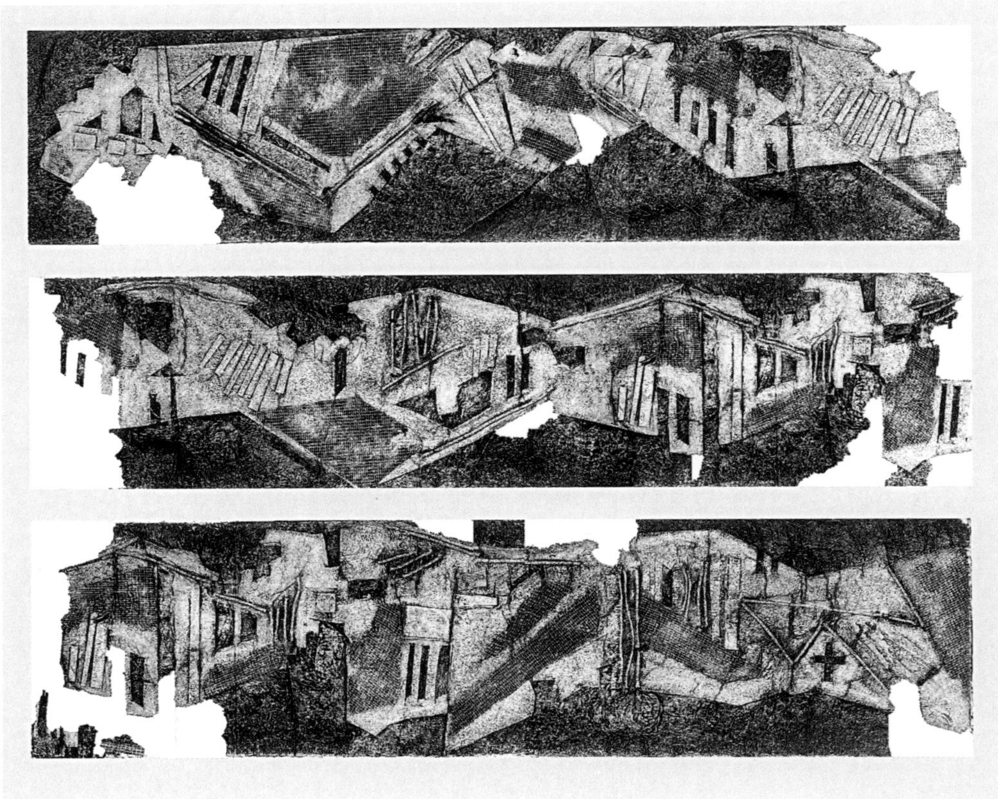

Emma Willemse, *Walking Amongst the Ruins*, collagraph, ink on paper, 2023

Once Emma is happy with the printing plate, she will apply a thin varnish-like shellac to seal and preserve it before applying the silkier intaglio ink. This will be rubbed away with a rag to create lighter areas, and allowed to gather in other places to add tone and depth. The damp paper is placed between the inked plate and layers of wool blankets on the printing press. When rolled through the press, this will push the paper into the textured plate to collect the ink and emboss the print. The final print is then photographed and digitally manipulated to create the end result.

TRY IT YOURSELF

Experiment with textured surfaces

Experiment with shiny materials like aluminium foil for areas of highlights. Rough materials like sandpaper are good for dark areas.

Everyday objects can provide patterning

Patterns can be picked up from pre-cut paper doilies, fruit netting or dressmaking trim. PVA glue can be used to attach these materials.

Printing

To get a good print from a collagraph, you will need a printing press for pressure and slightly damp printing paper which will be soft enough to press into the hollows and ridges to pick up all the textures and tone.

Inks

The oilier nature of intaglio printing ink is more suitable, as you will want to move the ink around and be able to rub it away on the shinier surfaces to make areas of lighter tone. If the paper is too dry, the print will be faint and the lines broken; if the paper is too wet the ink will spread and bleed and the lines will lose definition.

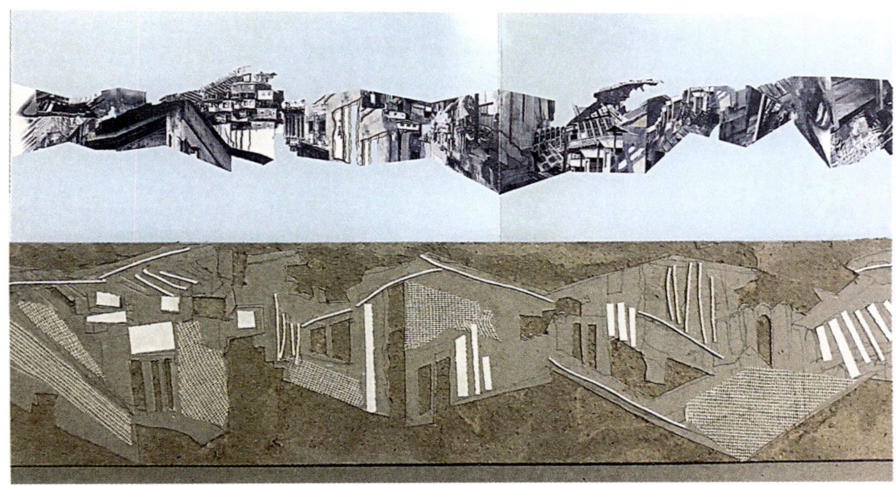

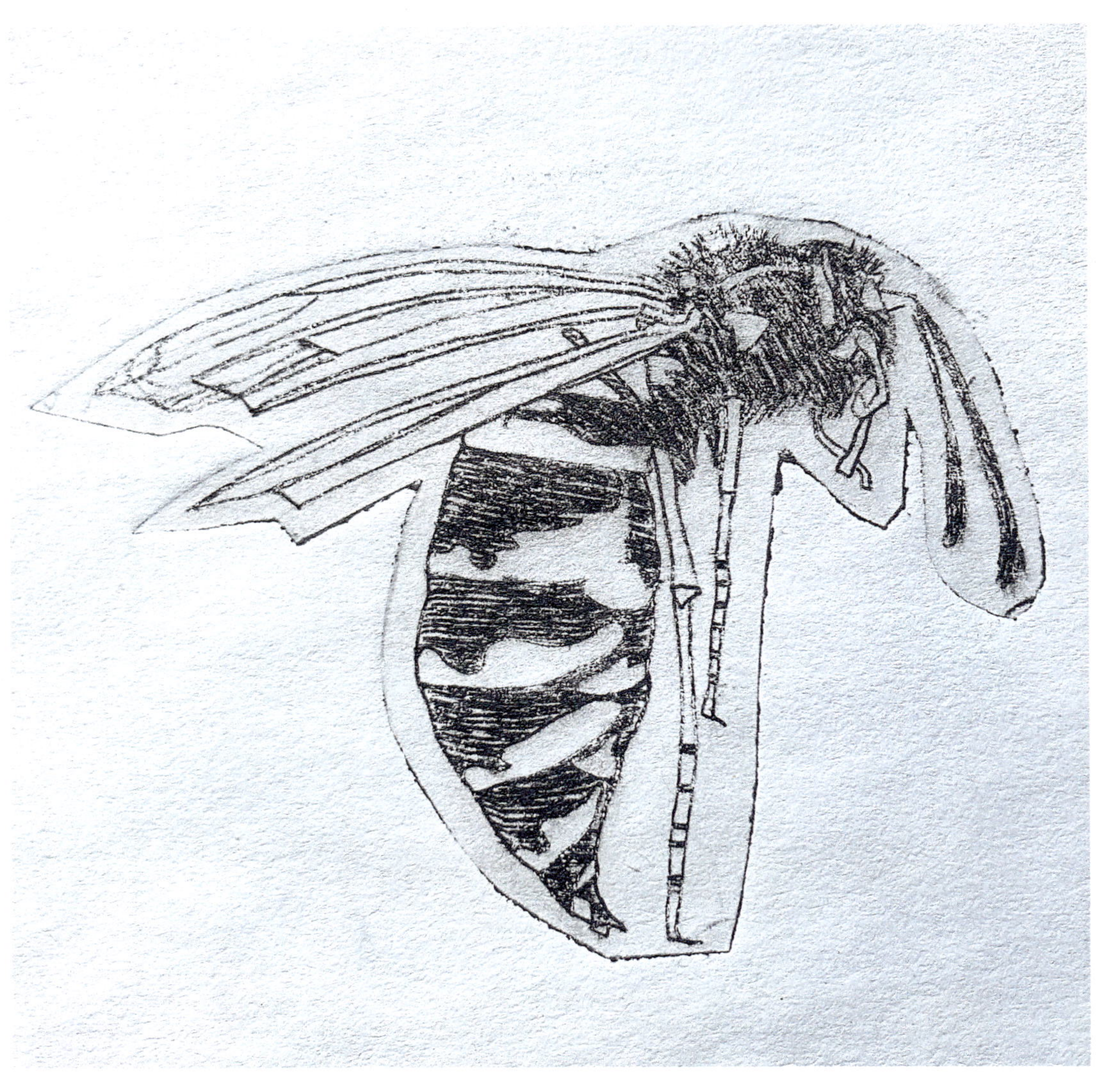

Eve Blackwood, *Wasp*, drypoint intaglio print, intaglio ink on watercolour paper, 2024

DRYPOINT

Drypoint is a very straightforward form of intaglio printing. It works on the simple premise that if the shiny surface of the printing plate is soft enough, you can make a deep scratch with a sharp point to create incisions which will hold the printing ink. Soft plastic like the material used to make milk containers or plastic document folders is a good choice for a printing plate. Here, the foil-backed lid of a food container has been used.

TRY IT YOURSELF

1. Draw the lines you want to print with a sharp point of a compass. To build up tone, draw lots of lines close together to create areas of hatching.

2. Rub a little ink into the plate as you are drawing to check the weight of the lines. Once you're happy with your plate, put it aside so you can prepare the printing paper.

3. Using a printing paper that is strong enough to take the embossing without ripping (330gsm in this case), quickly submerge it in water and then leave it to one side while you ink up the printing plate. If the paper is too wet, put it between two pieces of blotting paper so it dries out a little.

4. Inking up the plate is a creative process in intaglio printing. You can vary the mixtures of colours that you use, which areas you wipe clean to create highlights, and where you leave ink on the surface to create a darker tone. Once you are happy with the inking, you can place the plate on the printing bed with the paper on top. Printing presses usually have a thick blanket or two of wool which distributes the pressure evenly across the print.

5. After applying the pressure using the press you can peel the paper back to reveal the print.

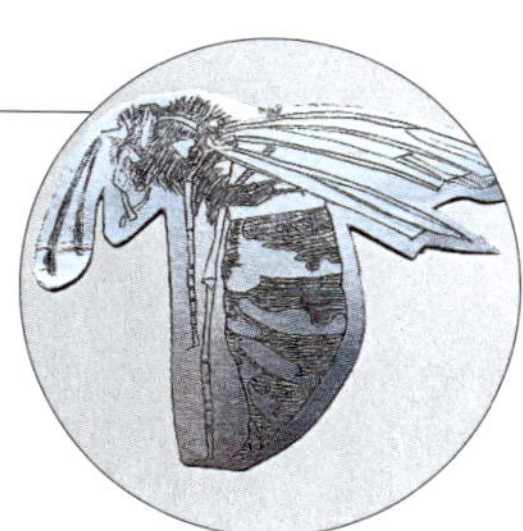

When the paper is too dry, the ink appears very faint.

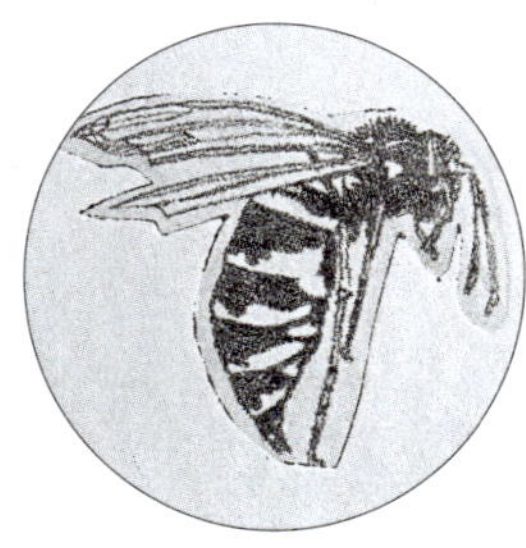

When the paper is too wet, the ink bleeds.

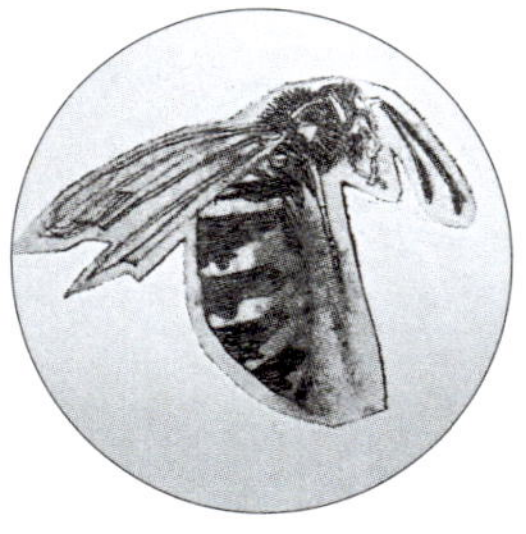

DEVELOP YOUR MARK MARKING

Etching is the art of scratching into metal that is covered in an acid-resistant coating. It is then placed into an acid bath which eats into the exposed, scratched metal to deepen these incisions and create lines on the printing plate. Tone can be added by hatching, aquatint (which is the application of acid-resistant resin) or allowing ink to stay on the surface of the plate before printing.

This etching, by Anthony Connolly, is a stunningly beautiful example of how this form of printing can capture the countless marks that have come together to form this study of a person's head. Anthony uses a great variety of marks: tight groups of short, hatched lines and cross-hatched lines that tell us about the texture and surface of the woman's face; delicate, tentative lines that describe her fly-away hair; and a bolder sensitive line that grows out of the dense darkness at the nape of her neck to flow around her head, describing the outline of her face and the curve of her chin. With this shading, he creates a sense of form, while the tilt of the head and the dreamy gaze give us a sense of her character. This really is a highly accomplished use of this medium.

TRY IT YOURSELF

Take inspiration from a Dutch master
Etching has a long and glorious place in the history of art. The prints of legendary Dutch artist Rembrandt van Rijn are an excellent place to look for inspiration when you are starting out with this printing medium.

Add energy with curves
Think about how you can use the marks you are making to describe the surface and form of the subject you have chosen. Bringing curves and flow to your line will add information and energy to your print.

Opposite: Anthony Connolly, *Octavia*, etching on copper, 2022

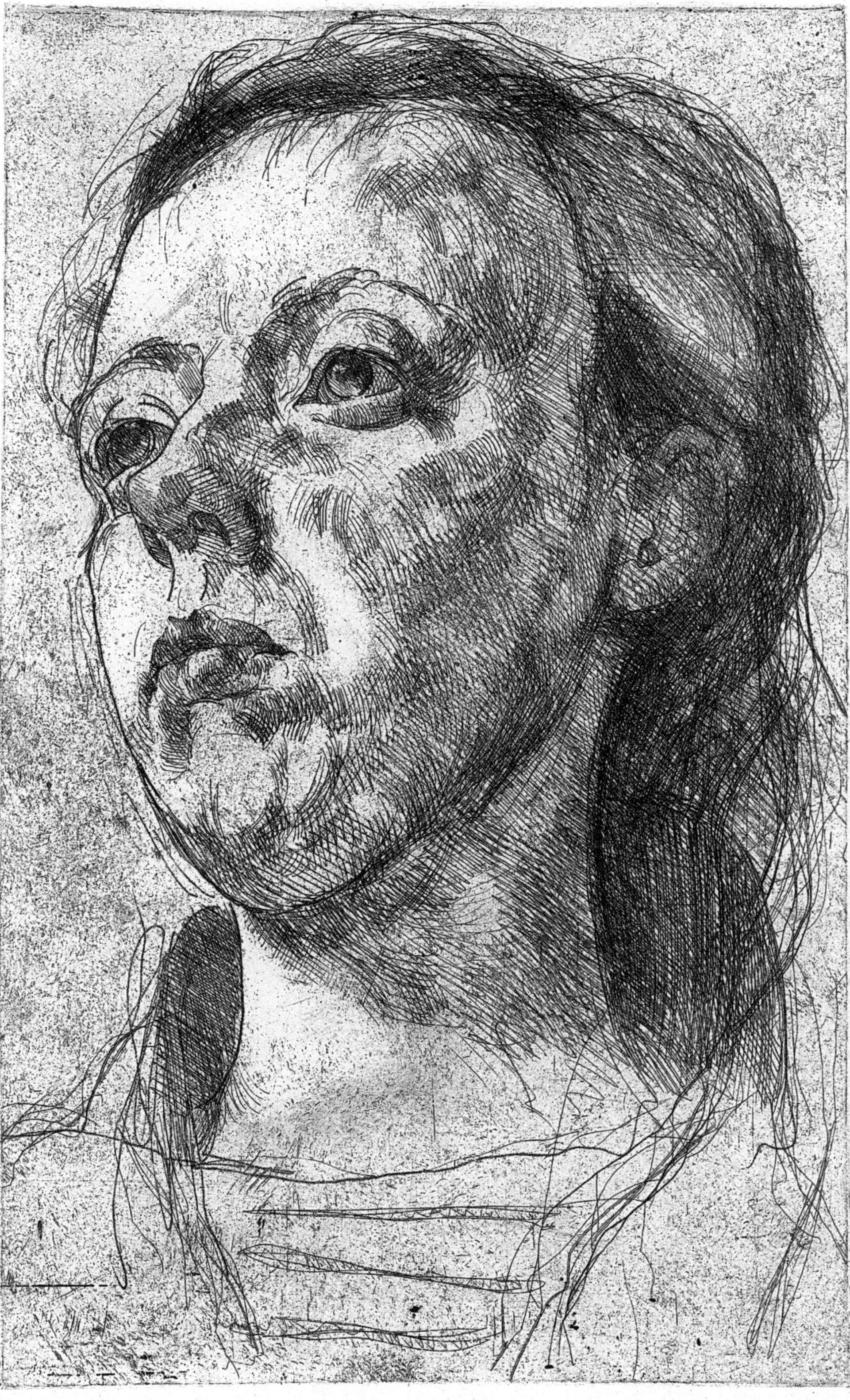

OTHER POSSIBILITIES

GO BIG OR GO HOME

When you work on a big scale you give yourself the ability to introduce another level of detail. This lino print is 180cm x 110cm, which is a lot of area to cover. Working at a large scale, Ade Adesina uses a mechanical carving tool to build up the wonderful variety of marks we can see here. This print celebrates the beauty and power of line, but also has the scale to allow the artist to create lines of great delicacy that sit quietly against dense areas of shadow. The intense texture in the rocks, plants and buildings is offset by the quiet areas of black at the bottom of the image, and this creates balance. Ade adds energy by leaving traces of marks in the sky that flow towards the vanishing point somewhere in the middle of his composition. This contrast of light and dark gives the landscape drama while the sky glows.

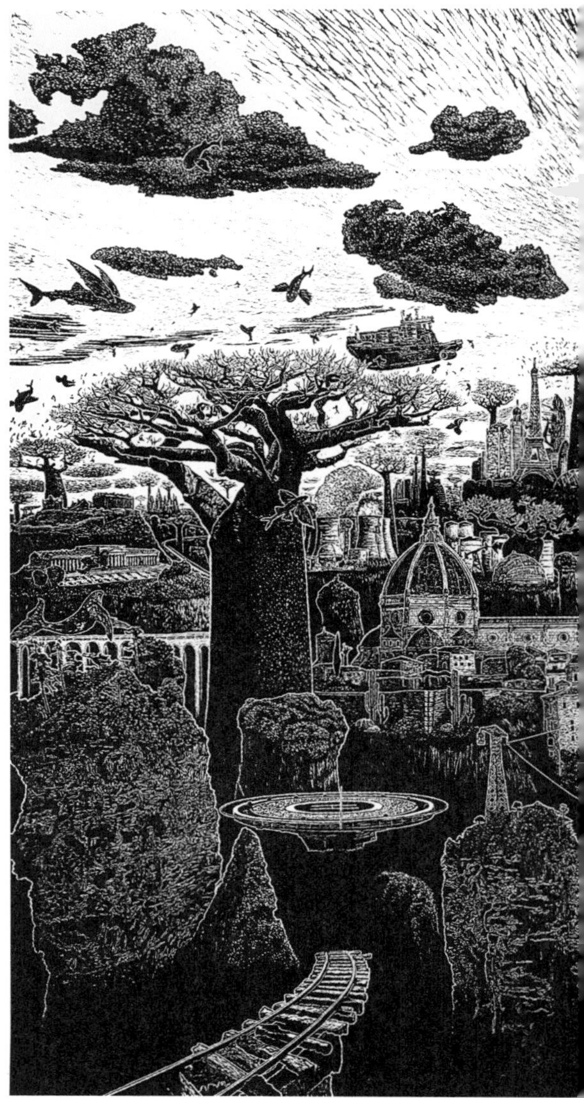

Tip

Start with one colour and experiment with how much you can communicate through simple lines. Consider the power of contrast: for example, a delicate white line will gain strength when placed against an uninterrupted block of colour.

Ade Adesina,
The Questions,
linocut, relief ink
on paper, 2015

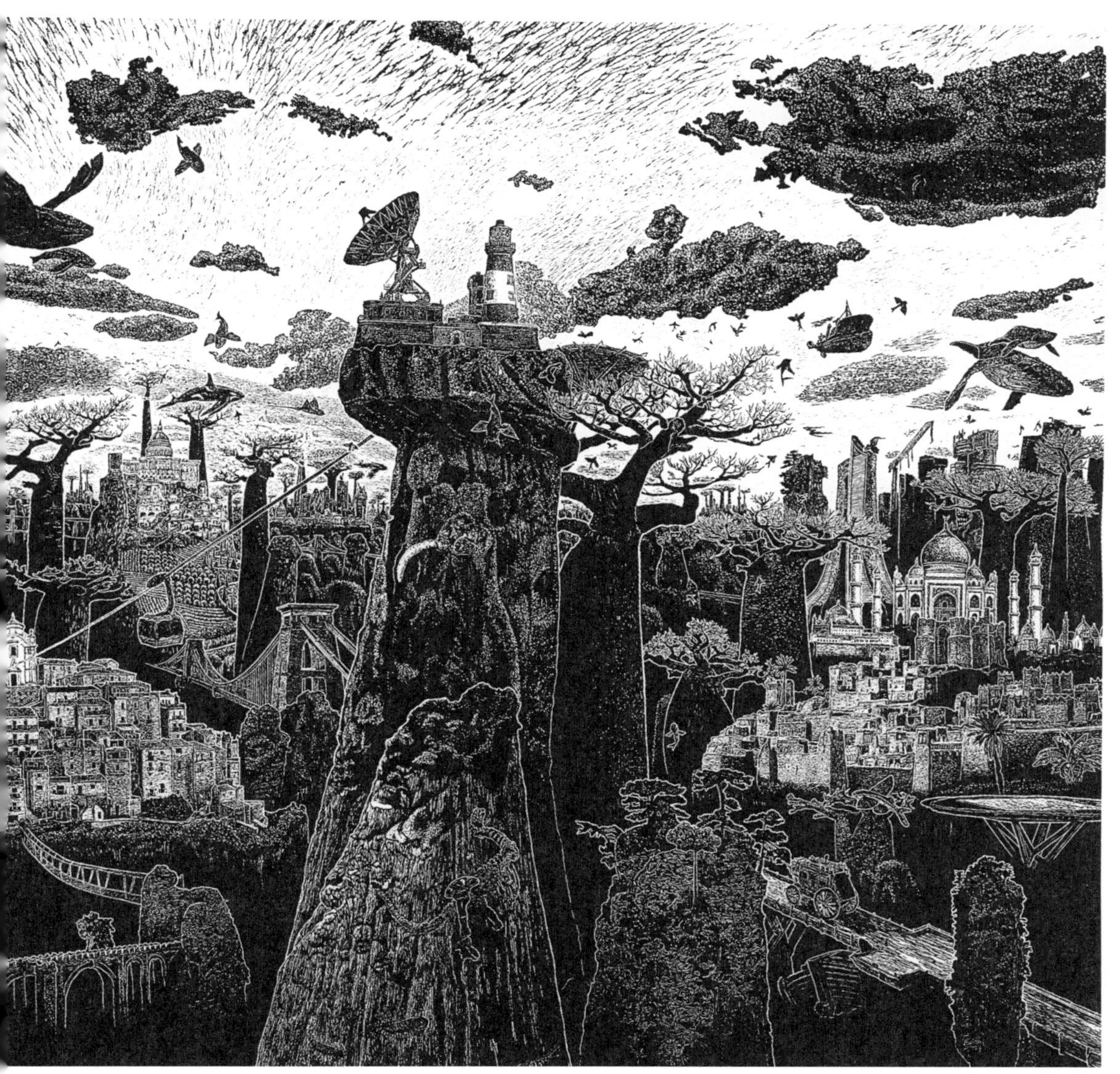

SCREEN PRINTING

Stencils and clever colour mixing are the key to a successful screen print. The process of screen printing involves a fine mesh screen pulled taut over a frame. Your printing ink will happily travel through this mesh when it is pulled along within the frame. To create your image, you have to prevent this happening in some areas of the screen. This can be done in a variety of ways: cutting a stencil from acetate which isolates the parts of the paper that you want the ink to reach; using a fluid which you can paint onto the areas where you want to block the ink; or photo exposure which transfers your image through UV light exposure onto photosensitized screens. To create a multicolour print like this one, you must plan ahead, deciding which colours can mix to create more complex colours and where you want to preserve the colour of the paper you are printing on.

Sara Ogilvie uses screen printing to create multiple prints (or editions) of her *Daddy Bear* print, which has a wonderful fluidity reminiscent of the monoprints we have looked at. This is masterful printmaking using halftones to create translucency; blocks of colour to give solidity to her sturdy protagonist; strong contrast to evoke the nighttime scene; offsetting (see page 105) to show the light spilling from the cottage door as it hits Daddy Bear's back; and subtle colour differences to describe the bark of the twiggy silver-birch trees. The way the smoke is painted keeps the smooth, flowing look of Sara's brushstrokes, giving the print a cloudy inkiness. The different techniques used in this image show the possibilities offered by this process.

Opposite: Sara Ogilvie, *Daddy Bear*, screen print on paper, 2007

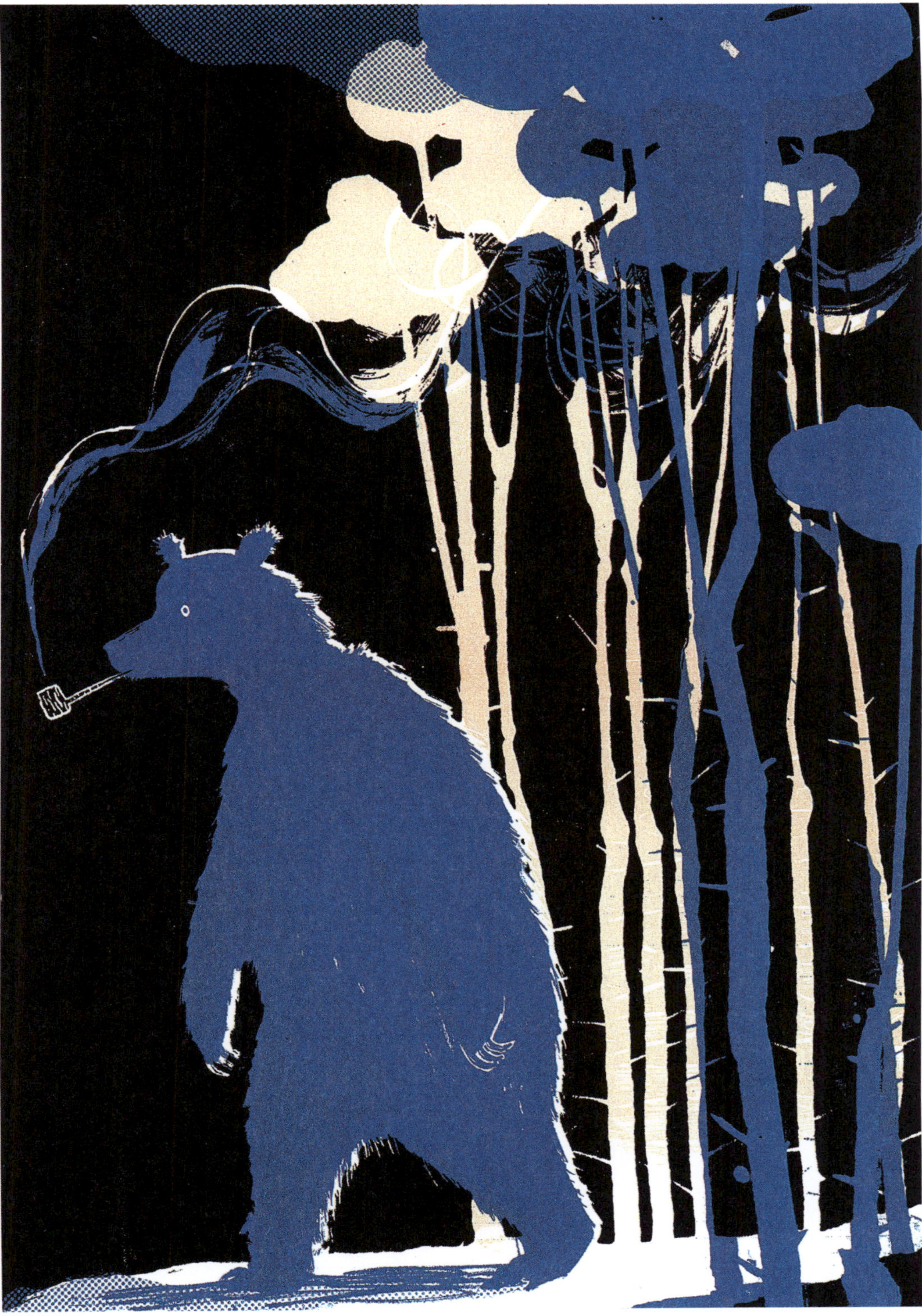

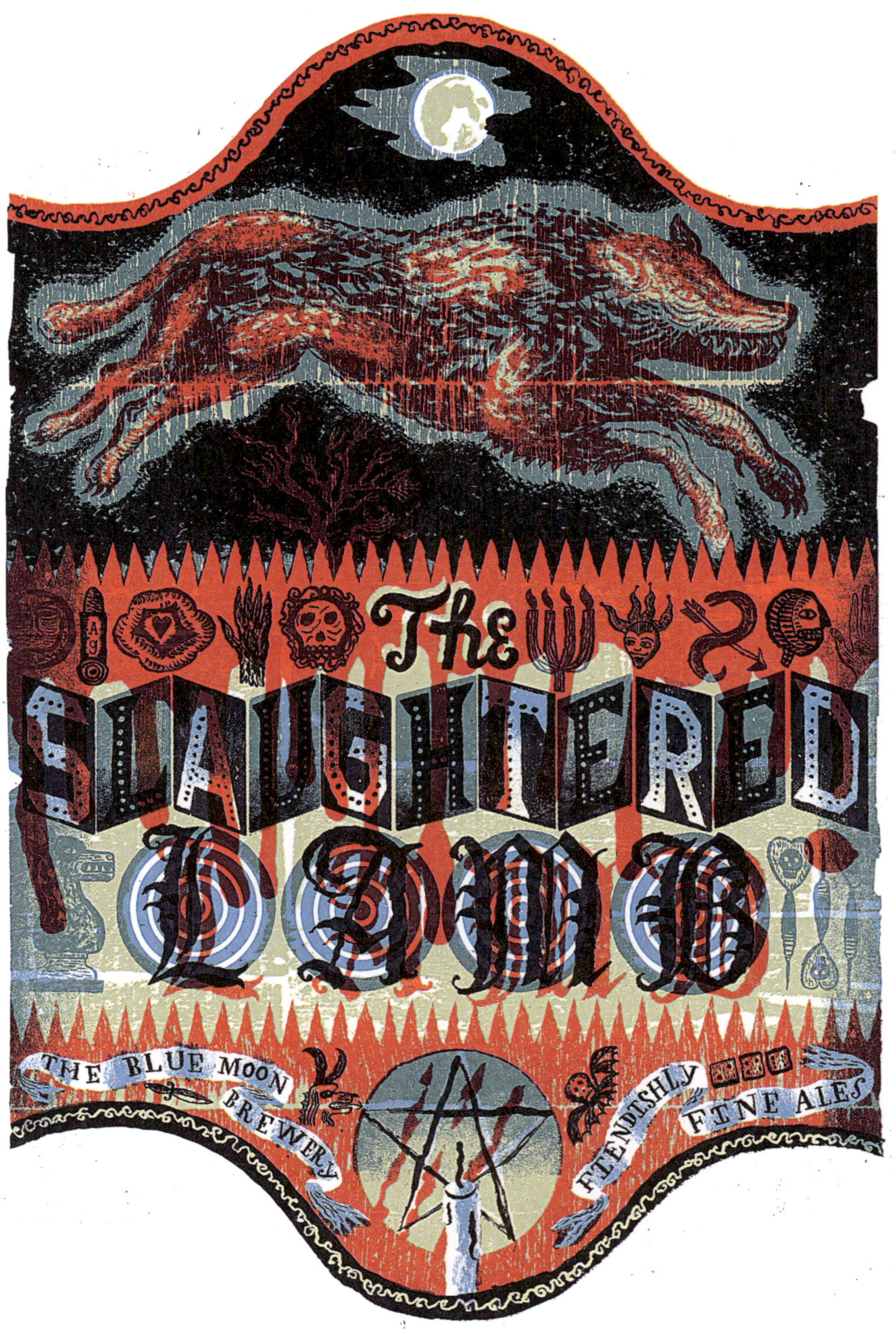
The
SLAUGHTERED
LAMB
THE BLUE MOON BREWERY
FIENDISHLY FINE ALES

CELEBRATE IMPERFECTION

Offsetting is when the layers of a multicolour print are not neatly lined up or 'registered', so that each colour is slightly out of sync with the previous one. When it is unintentional, it can cause visual confusion and spoil a print, but it has exciting possibilities when used deliberately.

Jonny Hannah has purposefully offset some of the printing in his pub-sign-inspired screen print, *The Slaughtered Lamb*. Careful not to overdo it, he offsets the printing around the words which gives the image a liveliness and energy. By carefully lining up the other parts of the design, however, the print is still readable. This is a nod to industrial printing processes where the register slipped over a large print run, so mass-produced printed goods like newspapers and comics often ended up with colour blocks that were out of sync with the outline they were intended to fill.

Offsetting creates a layering effect which Jonny has used throughout his design. We can see the red overlay dripping down towards the word lamb from the werewolf above which brings a narrative element to this image. With the five-pointed star and candles, he is harking back to folklore traditions of mythical beasts roaming the dark moors, preying on innocent lambs.

TRY IT YOURSELF

Consider the edges

The outline of this print is one of the key elements of the design, evoking a traditional pub sign swinging in the wind. Think about the edges as well as the interior of your print. What possibilities might they bring?

Visual clues

Creating a grainy texture in the lower layers of the print, including a distinct break under the werewolf, suggests a join in the wood that is used to construct the pub sign. Subtle visual clues like this can bring added interest to your prints.

Opposite: Jonny Hannah, *The Slaughtered Lamb*, four-colour screen print on paper, 2010

PRINTED OBJECTS

Natalia Ros has found an effective way of using her carved lino blocks to create beautiful pieces of ceramic that preserve all the subtleties of her lino block in the same way an embossed print would do. The range of tones that are produced in the shiny glaze give these plates the same slippery texture as the fish that she was inspired by.

These lovely platters have been embossed by pressing an uninked lino-printing plate into the soft surface of the clay. The glaze has then been allowed to pool into the depressions created by the embossing so, when fired, it really shows off the intricate patterns of the scales.

Tip

There are ways you can use your printing blocks to create a range of decorative objects. We have already looked at printing onto fabric, but that is just the tip of the iceberg. With the proper surface preparation, you can print onto many surfaces, including wood or walls, frames and light shades, or metal and glass.

Opposite: Natalia Ros, *Tuna*, linocut on ceramic, high-temperature stoneware, 2022

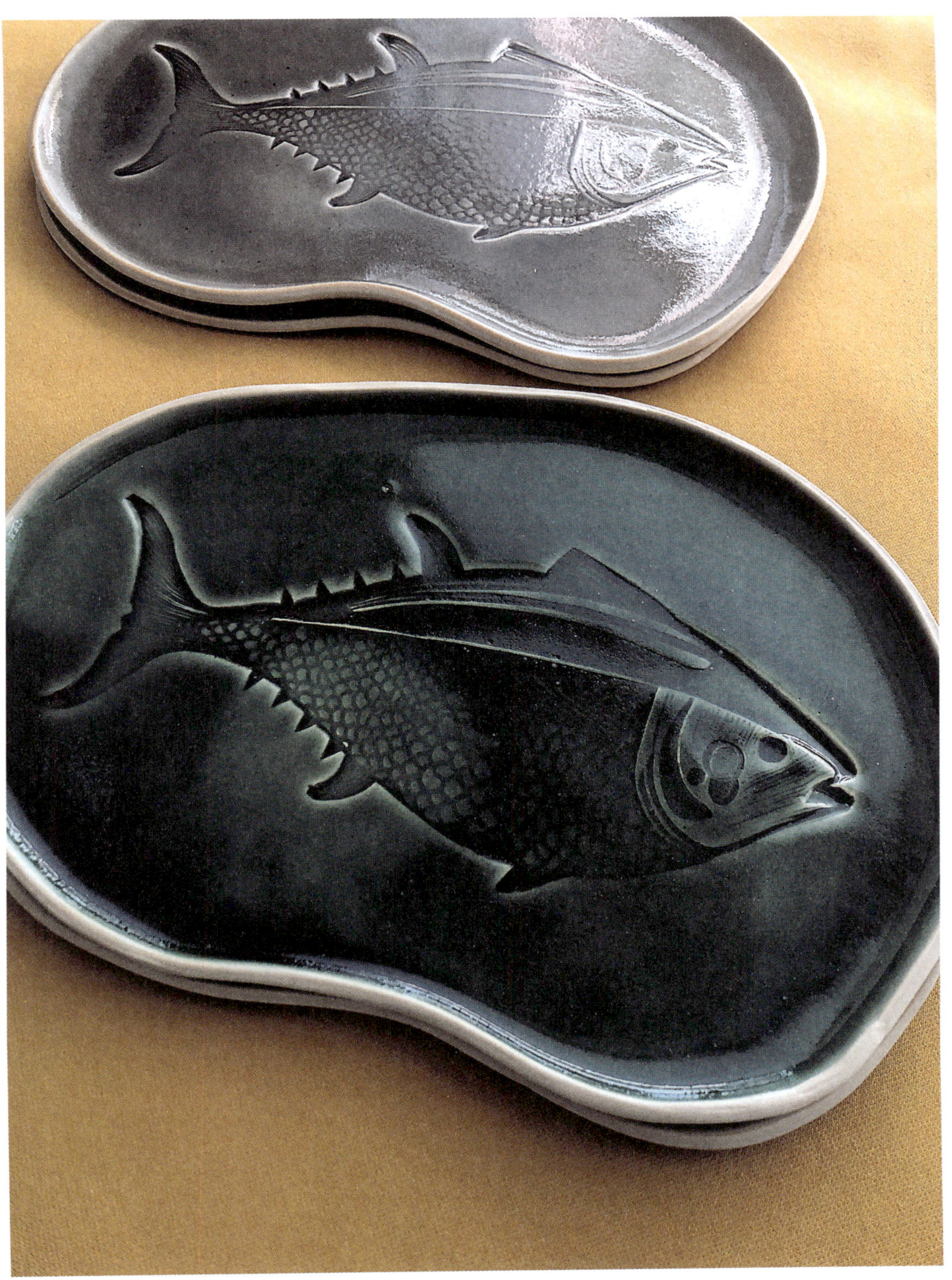

MIX YOUR MEDIA

Delita Martin shows how printmaking can be woven in amongst other means of artistic expression to create a rich and evocative piece of image-making. Her powerful central figure is described in black charcoal and white acrylic paint, while magical circles float in the air around her suggesting another, less tangible, part of our world. The dreamy look on her face suggests that these elements are the incarnation of her thoughts and daydreams. Her inner world is expressed in a wonderful variety of patterns, materials and symbols.

The relief-printed circles add texture in a light tone to the simple blue backdrop, while the embroidered circles of handmade paper on the woman's dress provide complex patterns of warm reds, with a central motif of rich gold suns nestling in the middle. Perhaps these beautiful patterns are a suggestion of the character's ancestral heritage. The addition of these elements to an already powerful portrait adds a fascinating insight into her mindset and mood.

The recurring motif of the circle helps to hold the overall design together. The consistent size of the large background circles means that, although they are sometimes split into two different media, they read as a complete circle. This circle motif is then repeated in smaller sizes on the arms of the figure.

Opposite: Delita Martin, *Blue Stars*, relief printing, charcoal, acrylic, liquid gold leaf, decorative papers and hand stitching, 2020

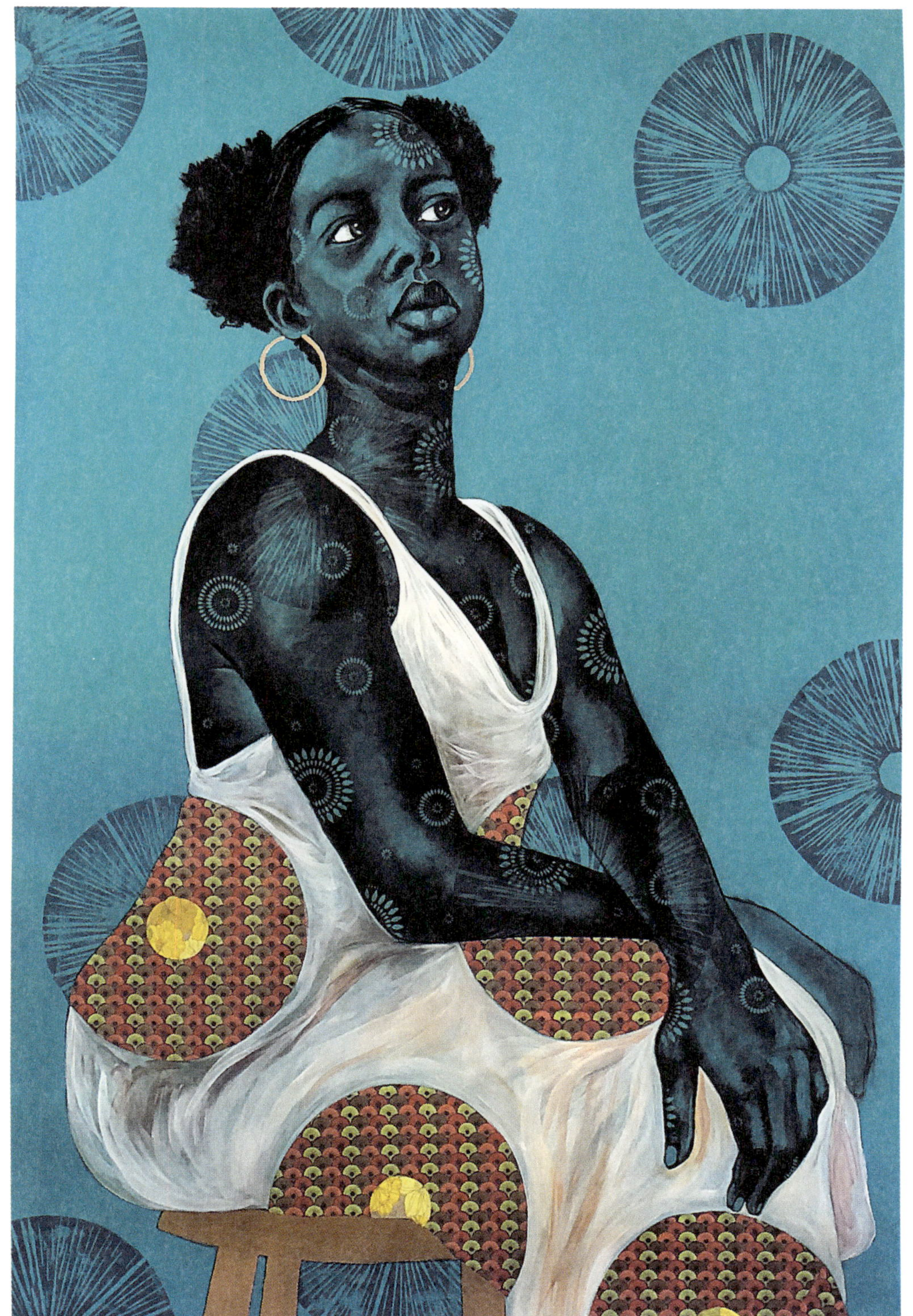

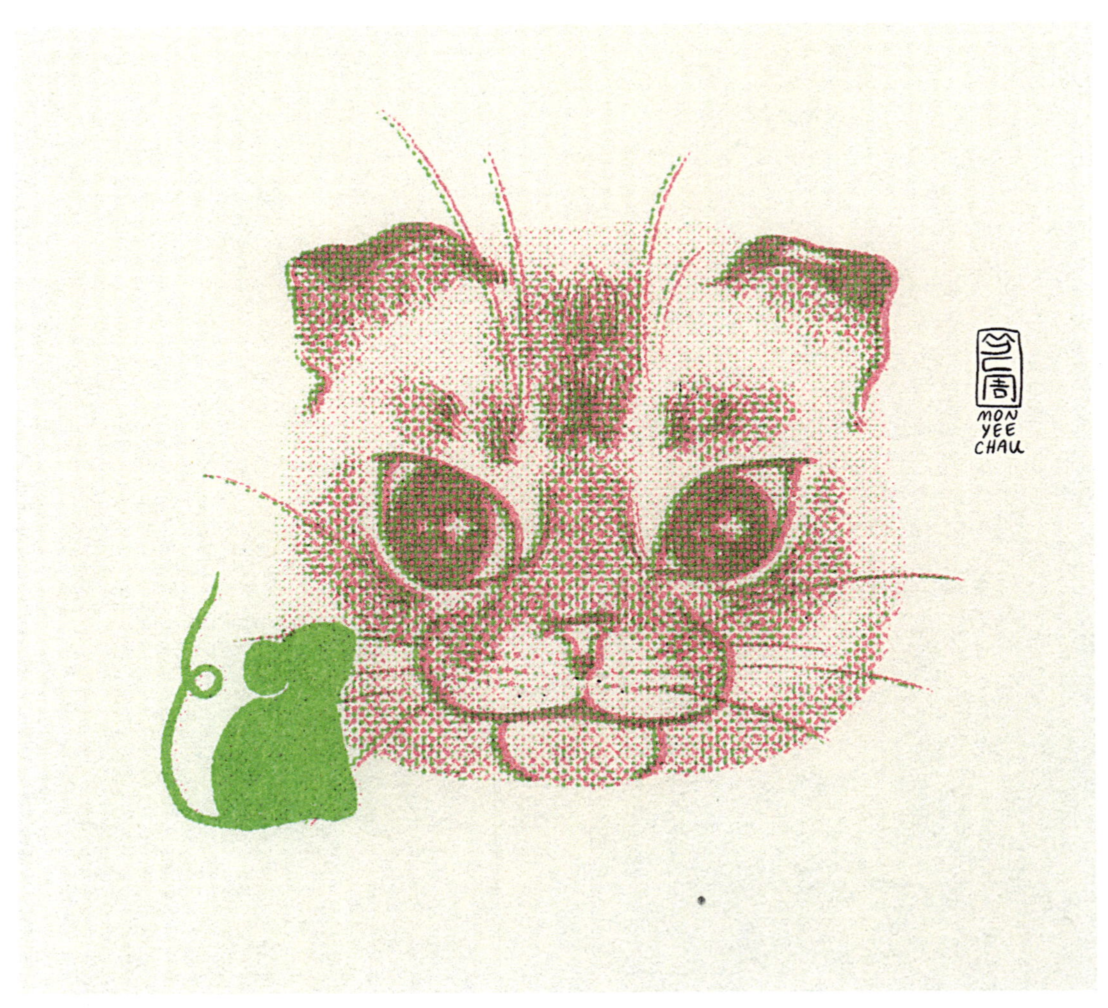

Monyee Chau, Cat and mouse animation frame, risograph on paper, 2024

EXPLORE OTHER PROCESSES

As I mentioned at the start of this book, printmaking has been around for millennia and there are many ways to create a printed image. Joining a print workshop will allow you to access wonderful techniques such as stone lithography, which uses the antipathy between grease and water to produce prints that retain the freshness of the original hand-drawn design. Aquatint, photogravure, engraving or working at large scale using lino or screen prints might also be possibilities. But one of the best reasons to join a workshop is to see what everyone else is making and to learn from them. Nothing happens in a vacuum. If you hit a wall creatively, one of the best things to do is get out there amongst other creative people and be inspired by learning a new technique or experimenting with a process in a new way.

Artist Monyee Chau has been experimenting with the possibilities of risographs, making a sequential series of printed images and filming them to create an animation. The misregistration of the colours gives the image a retro comic-strip look which suits the familiar pairing of cat-and-mouse characters. The slight variations in the printed frames give the film the look of an old flipbook.

TRY IT YOURSELF

Printing courses
Explore the possibilities of local workshops or colleges. Many places will allow you open access after you have completed some introductory technical courses.

Online courses
There are also online courses that will introduce you to new techniques or approaches to printmaking you may not have considered.

APPENDIX

MEET THE CONTRIBUTORS

Adam Larkum
www.adamlarkum.com
Adam Larkum studied illustration and animation, and received a BA followed by an MA from Edinburgh College of Art, Scotland. He then went on to work in the TV games and animation industry. He loves drawing and in 2000 he began freelancing as an illustrator and never looked back. Over the years, he has built up a variety of clients, working in publishing, editorial and advertising, as well as designing characters for television and working on iPad and iPhone book apps.

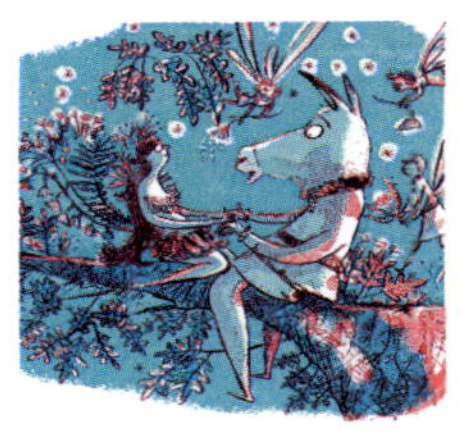

Ade Adesina
www.adeadesina.com
Ade Adesina, born in Nigeria in 1980, is a full-time artist based in Aberdeen, Scotland. Ade studied printmaking at Gray's School of Art, Aberdeen, and is a Royal Scottish Academician, member of The London Group and Associate Member of The Royal Society of Painter-Printmakers. Ade's work is a visual commentary on the ideas of ecology and our ever-changing world. He is a traditional printmaker, painter and sculptor who combines cultures and produces work that makes people reflect on the past, present and future.

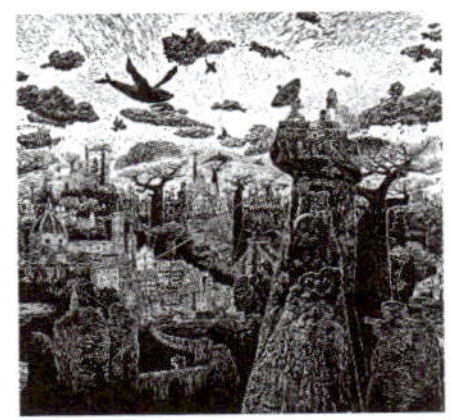

Amanda Outcalt
www.amandaoutcalt.com
Amanda Outcalt is a mixed-media printmaker living and working in Washington, D.C., USA. Her artwork is in private collectors' homes worldwide, including a piece in the permanent collection of the Virginia Museum of Contemporary Art. Outcalt combines her shaped intaglio copper plates with painting, hand stitching, gold leafing and pencil drawing to convey narratives about community and relationships.

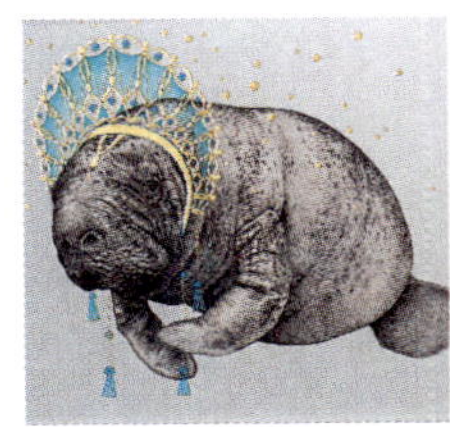

Anthony Connolly
www.anthonyconnolly.co.uk
Anthony Connolly is President of the Royal Society of Portrait Painters. His work is represented in many public collections, including the Royal Collection and several Oxbridge colleges. Drawing is central to his thinking and etching has been integral to the expression of that thought ever since he learned to etch when a student at Goldsmiths. Anthony's work has received many accolades, such as The Prince of Wales' Award for Portrait Drawing and The AXA Award for Drawing. His work is supported by Arts Council England.

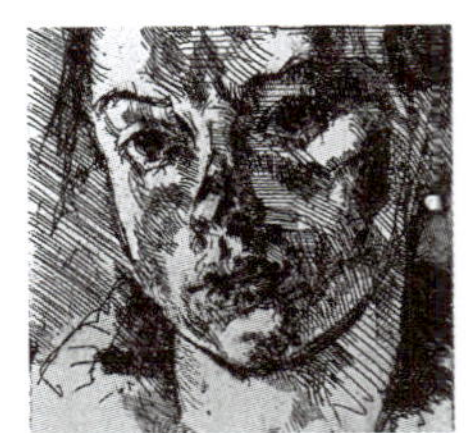

Asimina Hollingworth
@asimina_hollingworth
An avid image-maker and sequential artist, Asimina Hollingworth's work revolves around narrative and storytelling - explored through her autobiographical comics documenting the ever-so-mundane yet colourful and characterful interplay. She pushes this form through her love of experimentation, taking forms and elevating them to rather surreal dimensions: for instance, a multi-sensory comic-reading installation. The love of comics, characters and play drives Asimina's work.

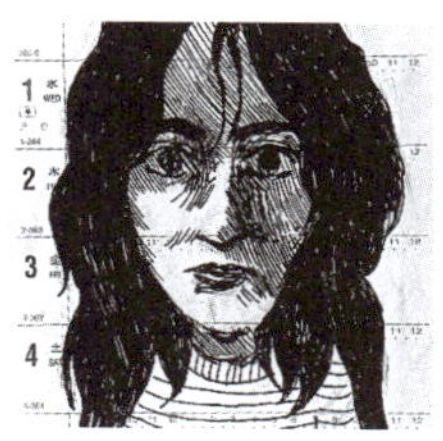

Brenda Holtam
www.brendaholtam.com
Brenda Holtam is a figurative painter and a teacher. She works in oils, watercolour, gouache and a wide range of drawing media. Brenda graduated from Falmouth School of Art and the Royal Academy Schools, and was elected a member of the Royal Watercolour Society. Her work is based on strong drawing skills and a fascination with colour harmony.

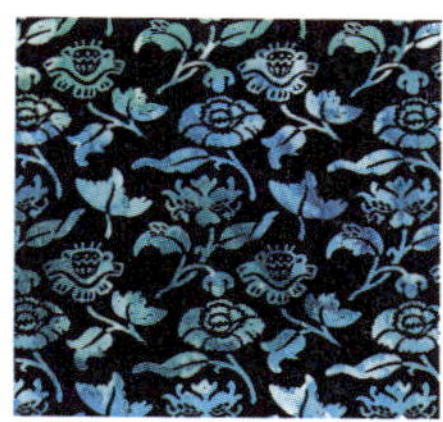

Bryan Christopher Baker
@stukenborgpress
Bryan Christopher Baker is a printmaker from Grayson, Georgia, USA. He has been doing traditional letterpress work for over 20 years, specialising in the use of hand-set type to create custom posters, limited-edition prints and various other kinds of ephemera. He keeps up with the modern times using photopolymer plates when needed, but he is better known for doing projects that use other materials on his presses, including actual dice. Printing directly from physical objects on the bed of the press, his designs capture the visual interactions of many simple shapes on the page. Bryan received his BFA in Printmaking from Ohio University and an MFA from the University of Tennessee. He has taught classes and workshops at many universities and craft schools.

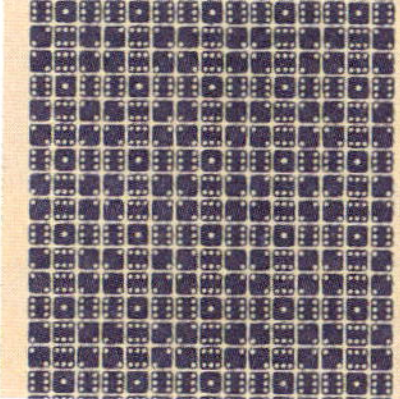

Claire Drury
@drury.claire
A textile artist, ceramicist and art teacher, Claire Drury strives to make every day creative. She collects treasure - feathers, old maps, fossils, broken pottery pieces - and is particularly interested in repurposing items discarded or unseen by others. This is reflected in her found-object pictures, quilts created from clothes and ceramics decorated with imprinted surface design.

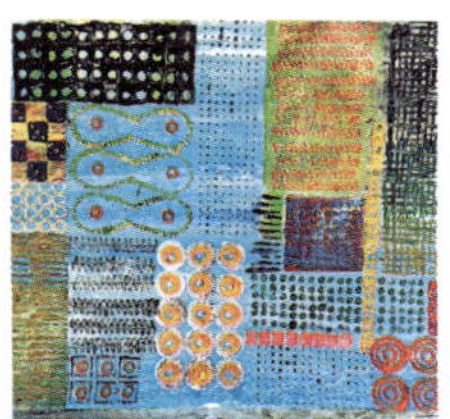

Clare Youngs
www.clareyoungs.co.uk
Clare Youngs studied graphic design at art college and worked in the industry for many years before changing direction and concentrating on illustration and collage. Clare loves texture and pattern in her work and uses paint, oil pastels, ink, pencil, wax resist and different printing methods to create a range of paper samples, which she cuts up and pieces together to make her artworks. Clare mostly draws inspiration from the world of animals. She prints using things gathered from the garden like pine needles and twigs, cut-up bits of erasers and sponges, and bits of cardboard - anything that makes a mark! In the last few years, Clare has discovered the joys of Gelli printing, with a whole new world of texture and pattern to be explored.

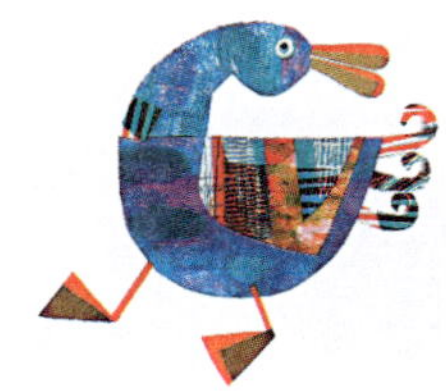

Delita Martin
www.blackboxpressstudio.com
Delita Martin is a master printer and accomplished artist. She holds a BFA in Drawing from Texas Southern University and an MFA in Printmaking from Purdue University. Formerly a member of the University of Arkansas at Little Rock's fine arts faculty, Delita devotes her time entirely to her artistic practice in the studio. Her prints, displayed in prestigious exhibitions and held in numerous private and corporate collections, delve into themes of Blackness, identity, spirituality and social justice. In 2024, Delita made history by becoming the first Black woman to have a solo exhibition in the Francine Kelly Gallery at the Featherstone Center for the Arts on Martha's Vineyard, a renowned creative hub for fostering artistic talent.

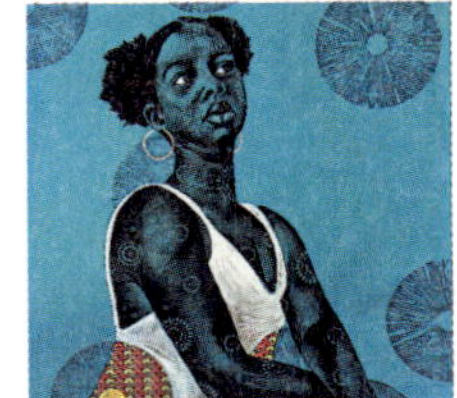

Emma Willemse
www.emmawillemse.co.za
Emma Willemse is a conceptual artist based in the small town of Riebeek Kasteel in South Africa. Exploring ideas about human experiences associated with loss and place, such as displacement and site-specific commemoration, Emma's art practice covers a wide range of media and techniques, including installations, painting, printmaking, photography, artist's books and film. She holds a Masters in Visual Arts from the University of South Africa, as well as qualifications in librarianship and psychology.

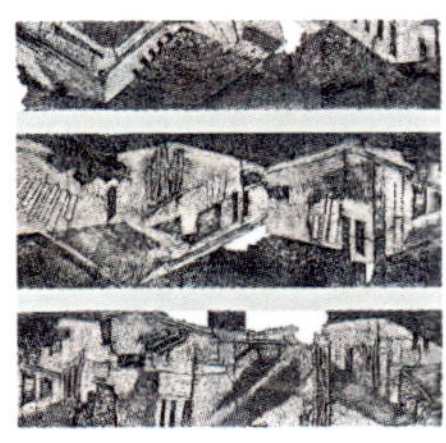

Georgina Bown
www.georgina-artist.co.uk
Georgina studied at The Chelsea School of Art in London and has been a professional artist for over 20 years. She specializes in steel sculpture, drawing and printmaking. Living near the coast in Scotland, Georgina has become fascinated by the nautical monsters of the sea, both man-made and organic. Mark making and experimenting is essential to her process of depicting the scale of these monsters. Georgina was selected to exhibit at the Masters of Monoprinting at the Bankside Gallery, London.

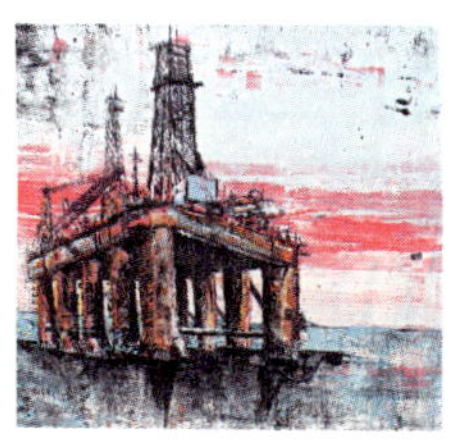

Howard Vie
www.hvie.co.uk
Howard Vie is an architectural illustrator inspired by the detail of classical landscapes and buildings. He trained in drawing with visionary artist Cecil Collins RA and worked in the office of eminent modern classical architect Julian Bicknell, where he had a technical role, as well as illustrating many of Julian's proposed projects. His illustrations of existing buildings were used in several of the Conservation Area Studies published by Richmond Council in London.

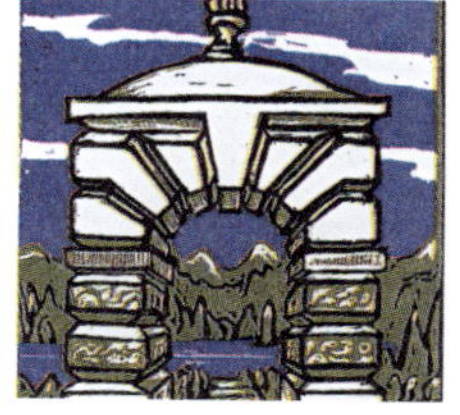

Imi Maufe
www.imimaufe.com
After studying Multi-Disciplinary Printmaking at the University of the West of England, Bristol (2004), visual artist Imi Maufe has been involved in residencies, artistic research, exhibitions and collaborative curating. She is a co-founder of Codex Polaris and the Nordic Letterpress Network, artist-run collectives promoting artist books and letterpress in the Nordic countries. Imi experiments with print - mainly letterpress - through available facilities and to suit each project. She works at the Norwegian Printing Museum in Stavanger, Norway.

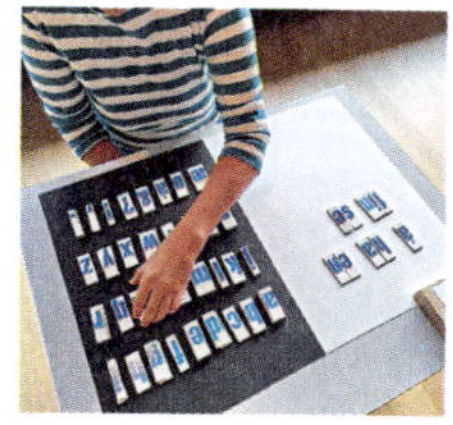

James Brown
www.pressedandfolded.com
Having trained as a textile and surface-pattern designer and then designed prints and graphics for menswear, James made the switch from fabric to printing on paper in 2007. Alongside his printmaking practice, James works commercially as an illustrator, both digitally and on the press. He has been commissioned for a variety of projects, including designing the iconic East End Trades Guild logo and, annually since 2010, designing the Foyle Young Poets Award poster and anthology. In 2017, Walker Books published *A World of Information*, which James illustrated. This became an international bestseller and has been followed by four more books in the series, also illustrated by James.

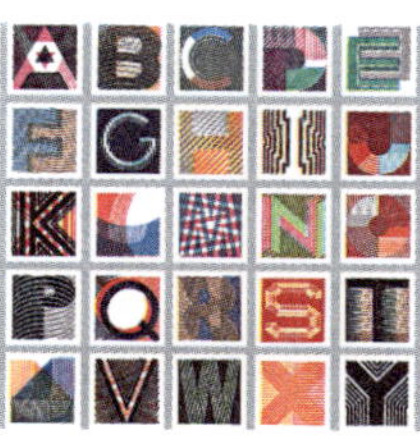

Jane Ormes
www.janeormes.co.uk
Jane Ormes is a multimedia artist who primarily works as a printmaker and ceramicist. She lives in Bristol, England, and works from her home studio. Primarily a screen printer, her prints exude her love of colour and mark making and often feature whimsical animals and elements of pattern. She has worked commercially with clients such as Ikea, Marks & Spencer and Nosy Crow. She has illustrated 11 children's books and keeps many journals of her observational drawings. Her work has been exhibited throughout the UK with many independent galleries.

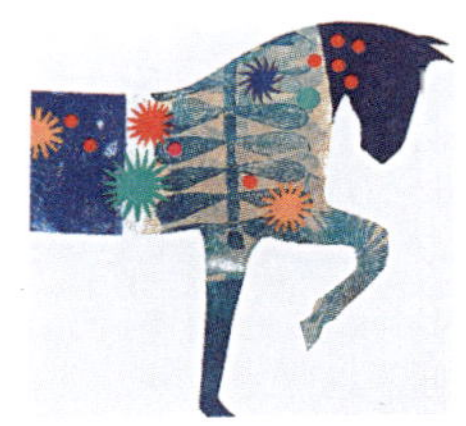

Jennifer Zee
www.ginkgozee.com
Jennifer Zee is a Chinese-American, San Francisco-based printmaker who prints distinctive nature- and geometry-inspired art from hand-carved blocks. Jennifer's designs are meticulous, often featuring intricate tessellations that incorporate concepts and aesthetics from her background as a scientific illustrator and biologist. Jennifer is an active artist and teacher in her local community. She is passionate about using her art to inform her audience about biodiversity and conservation, as well as social justice, with a focus on the Chinese-American experience.

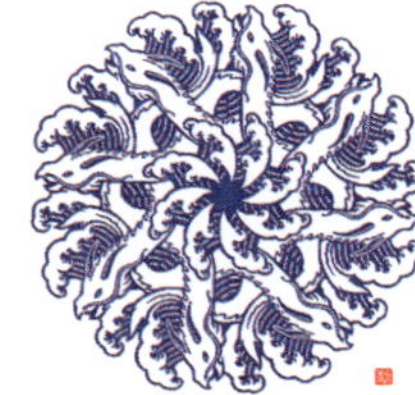

John Pedder
www.johnapedder.com
Woodcut printmaking slows John down, allowing him the time to put great industry into the simplest mark. For him, it also offers the magic of happenstance and unpredictability, which allows no end of inspiration and frustration - but, hopefully, mainly inspiration. John has decided to fully embrace only two dimensions (suggesting that three would appear greedy), so his work is right on the surface of the paper. He makes no apologies for being the polar opposite of the *Star Wars* special effects team, but doesn't believe that his design ability is any less sophisticated. He creates restriction to search for creativity, believing that restriction is actually very liberating.

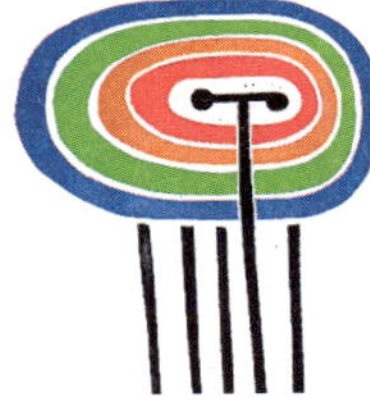

Jonny Hannah
www.heartagency.com
Jonny Hannah is a freelance illustrator. He has many passions, including the music of Hank Williams, hand-drawn lettering and the films of Jacques Tati. He has illustrated, written and assembled various books, including *Greetings from Darktown* and *Fast Cars & Ukuleles*. He also plays in a top beat combo, The Postmen, delivering urban folk anthems with council-estate choruses. Oh, and he enjoys the odd lycanthrope too, hence the pub sign enclosed in this fine volume.

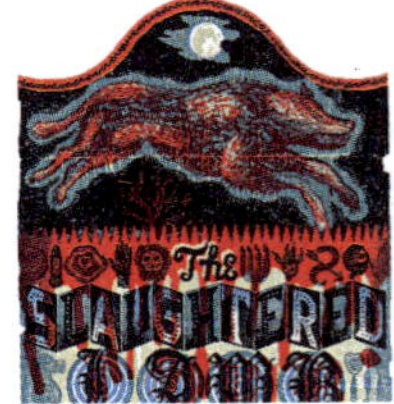

Karen Wicks
www.ghostbuildings.co.uk
Karen Wicks is a UK printmaker based in the Midlands. Her printmaking practice is inspired by derelict buildings and captures the presence and intrigue of these abandoned structures using intaglio print techniques. The Japanese notion of 'wabi-sabi' is central to her art practice, which celebrates beauty that is imperfect, impermanent and incomplete. The narrative of everyday and forgotten places inspires her to record these places using sustainable printmaking practices. Her work explores low-fi home-print techniques and uses recycled packaging that becomes fragile and disintegrates over time to reflect the subject matter of the 'ghost buildings' that inspire her.

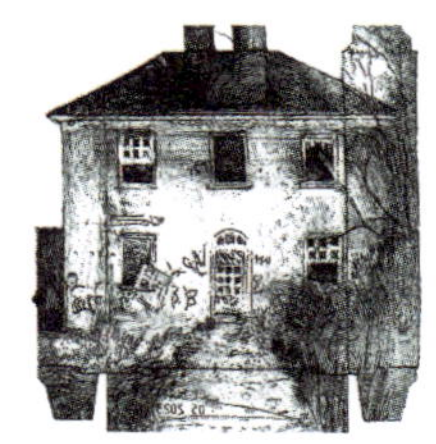

Kasey Golden
www.kaseygolden.com
After studying graphic design at Middle Tennessee State University, USA, Kasey moved to Canada (having closed the gap to her long-distance relationship by getting married). To keep herself productive and creative while she waited for her work visa, she started a YouTube channel, intending to become a freelance artist and share her illustrative process. Her YouTube videos took off and before she knew it she was officially a 'YouTuber', creating challenge videos and tutorials and growing an audience who shared her love for art.

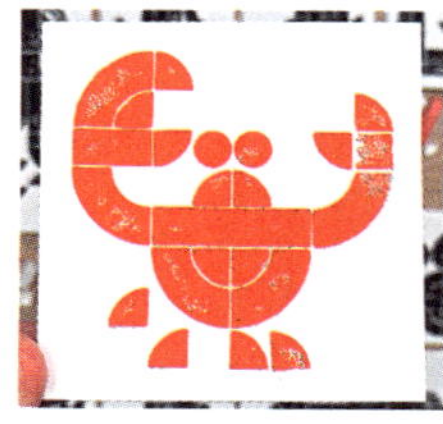

Koichi Yamamoto
www.yamamotoprintmakin.com
Koichi's prints explore themes of the sublime, atmosphere and fluid mechanics. His work ranges from meticulous copper engravings to large-scale monotypes. Recently, he has dedicated himself to making kites. Koichi studied at the Pacific Northwest College of Art in Portland, Oregon, USA, then moved to Kraków, Poland, and later to the Academy of Fine Arts and Design in Bratislava, Slovakia, to study copper engraving. He completed his MFA at the University of Alberta, Canada, and is currently a professor at the University of Tennessee in Knoxville, USA.

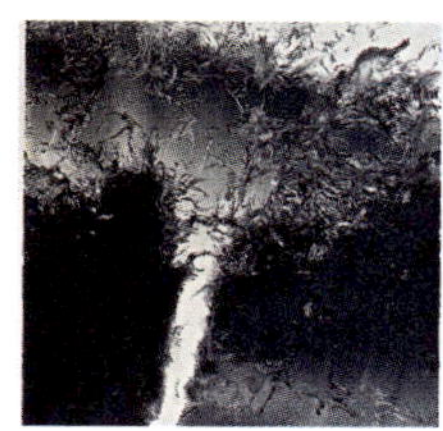

LaToya Hobbs
www.latoyamhobbs.com
LaToya Hobbs is an artist, wife and mother of two from Little Rock, Arkansas, USA, who is currently living and working in Baltimore, Maryland. She received her BA in Painting from the University of Arkansas at Little Rock and her MFA in Printmaking from Purdue University. Her work deals with figurative imagery that addresses the ideas of beauty, cultural identity and womanhood as they relate to women of the African diaspora. Through her mixed-media works she explores the idea of the 'matrix as art object', combining key elements from both her painting and printmaking practices.

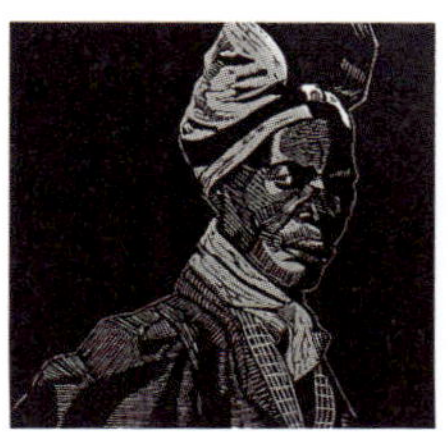

Laura Crehuet Berman
www.lauracrehuetberman.com
The work of Spanish-American artist Laura Crehuet Berman is grounded in earth science and the body. Berman has exhibited her work in numerous galleries and museums internationally and her prints are widely collected. She is a professor at Kansas City Art Institute, USA, and has been teaching in the printmaking department since 2002. In 2024, Berman was a Fulbright Senior Scholar at the University of Canberra, Australia.

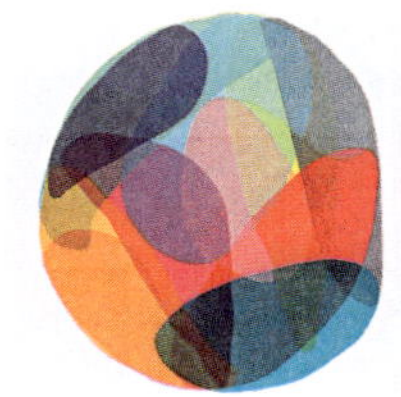

Lily Vie
www.lilyvie.com
Lily Vie is an illustrator and comic artist currently based in London. Using a combination of traditional and digital media, mainly watercolour and gouache, her work explores fantasy and the surreal, as well as the familiar and comforting. She draws inspiration from nature, ornamental design, typography and little creatures.

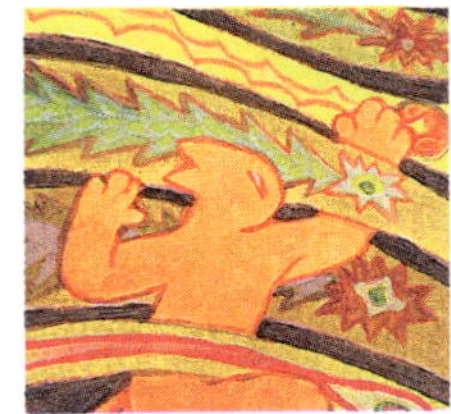

Marjorie Accarier
@marjorie_acc
Marjorie Accarier is an artist specialising in linocutting and etching. Her work in illustration offers reinterpretations of tarot archetypes, but is also inspired by mediaeval Christian-Orthodox iconographies and symbols and Jungian philosophy, with the idea that in everyone there is the sacred beyond religious dogmas. Stained-glass jewellery creations have also recently become part of her practice. She lives in Paris and works within the Paris Print Club collective.

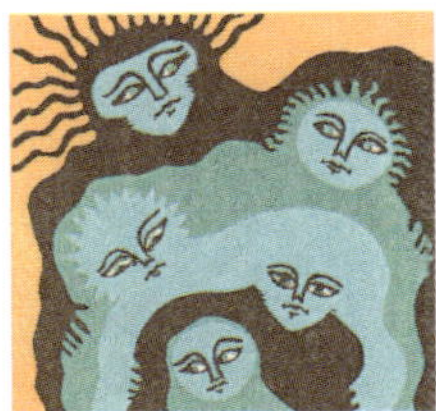

Matt Roussel
www.artzmatt.com
Matt Roussel was born in 1964 in the south of France. Having worked for a long time as an illustrator in publishing, the press and advertising, he travelled to Mongolia in 2015 and decided to devote himself mainly to wood engraving and ceramics. Over time, his work as an engraver evolved and he invented a unique art by painting previously engraved wooden boards in acrylic. His favourite themes are the relationships between people, animals and nature. He sells his works all over the world on his website and exhibits all year round in France and Europe at contemporary art fairs.

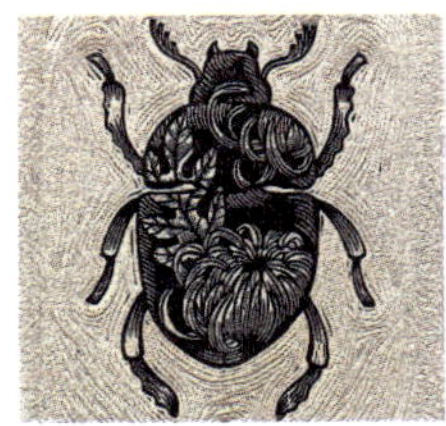

Monyee Chau
www.chinesebornamerican.com
Monyee Chau is an interdisciplinary Taiwanese/Chinese-American artist residing on the unceded lands of Coast Salish/Duwamish of the United States. They received their BFA from Cornish College of the Arts, and explore the ideas of healing and diaspora through labour in multiple processes of art. They are interested in intersections of identity and building community through shared food and storytelling.

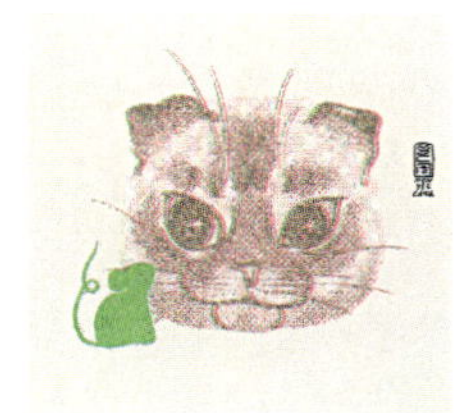

Natalia Ros
@nataliaros_ilustra
Natalia Ros is a Basque illustrator and printmaker based in Barcelona, Spain. She studied fine arts at the University of the Basque Country. All her illustrated projects are 100 per cent hand-printed with linocut. They are inspired by nature and especially by the sea. Natalia has her own shop/studio in the famous Sants neighbourhood in Barcelona. The tuna plate is a collaboration with Sanfangs, a Catalan ceramicist artist specialising in tableware for the best restaurants in the country.

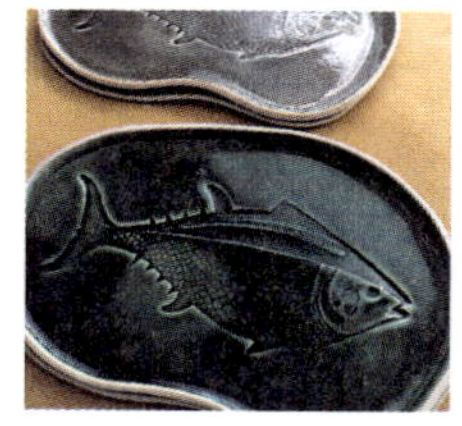

Patricia Hardmeier
www.patriciahardmeier.com
Patricia Hardmeier is a multi-disciplinary artist specialising in oil-based monotypes. She graduated from ArtCenter College of Design in Pasadena, California, USA, in 2000. Her monotypes have been exhibited at international venues and events. She is inspired by nature and influenced by her background in ballet and flamenco, exploring the expressive potential of printmaking through dynamic and intricate compositions.

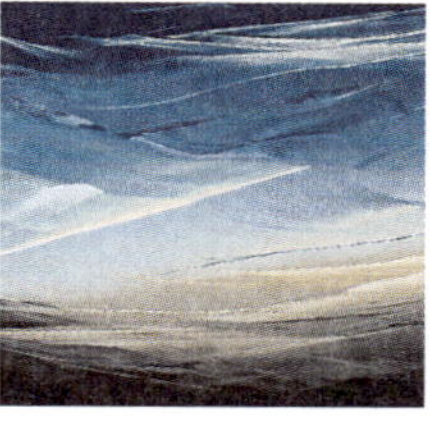

Paul Farrell
@paulfarrelldesign
Paul Farrell is a graphic artist and designer based in his home city of Bristol, England. After graduating in 1988, his creative career began in London as a graphic designer, specialising in brand design. Now self-employed, Paul is also an illustrator, author and printmaker. His world is continuously filled with shape and colour. Brought up on a diet of 1970s pop culture, pattern and graphic arts, his bold, colourful and geometric style translates his everyday into simple and playful imagery. Paul divides his home-studio time between graphic design and illustration and has been commissioned overseas and in Europe by Apple, HarperCollins, Paul Smith, Calvin Klein and the Hayward Gallery, London, for a variety of projects including stationery, art, packaging, fashion, retail, product design and publishing.

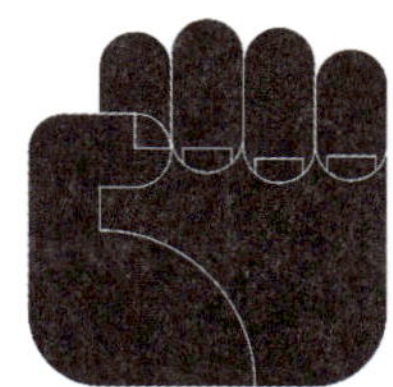

Rachel Newling
www.rachelnewling.com

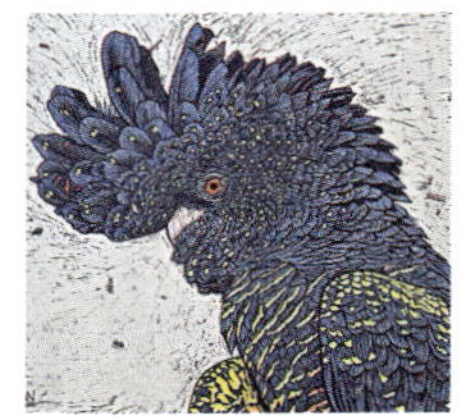

Rachel Newling is an established, independent artist who has been specialising in various printmaking techniques for many years and is a leading linocut artist. Born in the UK in 1956, Rachel grew up next to the beach near Padstow in Cornwall. Being out in nature was her main childhood pastime and she developed a keen interest in the creatures and landscape of that wild stretch of North Atlantic coast. Later, Rachel moved to London to attend art schools then made her way to visit family in Australia. After visiting a couple of times, she moved to Sydney permanently in 1982, choosing to again live near the water, this time in Sydney's Northern Beaches.

Raubdruckerin
www.raubdruckerin.de

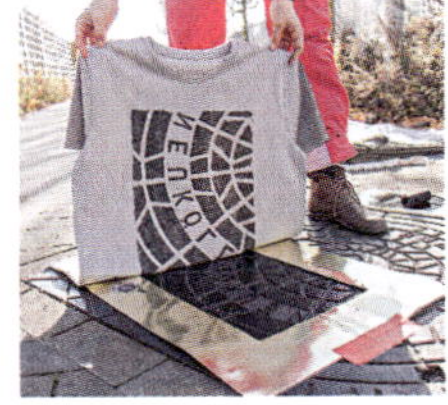

Raubdruckerin ('pirate printer') is the alias of artist Emma-France Raff as well as a brand. Since 2006, it has told stories through prints created from its surroundings. Manhole covers, concrete structures, street signs, leaves, fruit, cookies and more have all been used as printing plates, their surfaces receiving new life as they are transferred to paper and fabric.

Sara Ogilvie
www.saraogilvie.com

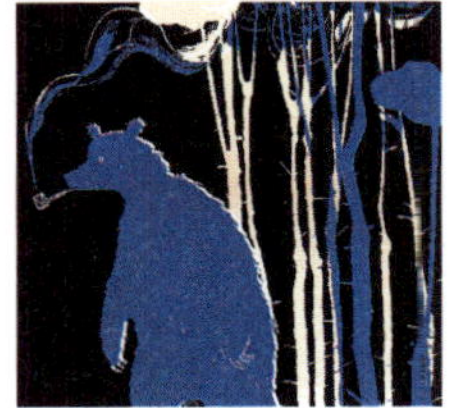

Sara Ogilvie is an artist, illustrator and lecturer from Edinburgh, now based in Newcastle upon Tyne, England. Drawing, mark making and storytelling are central to her work, and she has exhibited in both solo and group shows in the UK and abroad. Her published illustrations blend traditional print and digital methods. Collaborations include picture books with Anna Kemp, Julia Donaldson, Garth Jennings and Katherine Rundell. She has worked with The Folio Society on several titles, including Dodie Smith's *The Hundred and One Dalmatians*, which won a D&AD Pencil in 2018. Ogilvie's books have also been adapted for stage and television.

Saul Steinberg
www.saulsteinbergfoundation.org
Famed worldwide for giving graphic definition to the postwar age, Saul Steinberg (1914–1999) had one of the most remarkable careers in American art. While renowned for the covers and drawings that appeared in *The New Yorker* for nearly six decades, he was equally acclaimed for the drawings, paintings, prints, collages and sculptures he exhibited internationally in galleries and museums. Saul Steinberg crafted a rich and ever-evolving idiom that found full expression through these parallel yet integrated careers. He was a modernist without portfolio, constantly crossing boundaries into uncharted visual territory. In subject matter and styles, he made no distinction between high and low art, which he freely conflated in an oeuvre that is stylistically diverse yet consistent in depth and visual imagination.

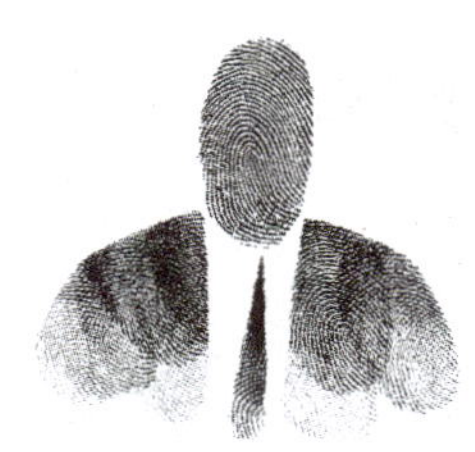

Steph Renshaw
www.stephrenshawprintmaker.com
Steph is a printmaker and print teacher based in Bristol, England. Her work draws on her own encounters with wildlife as well as her degree in environmental biology. She is in awe of nature and fascinated by it. She is intrigued by the relationship between humans and the rest of the natural world. Printmaking allows endless experimentation with her approach. She enjoys the variety of different processes and loves to play with colour and with positive and negative space.

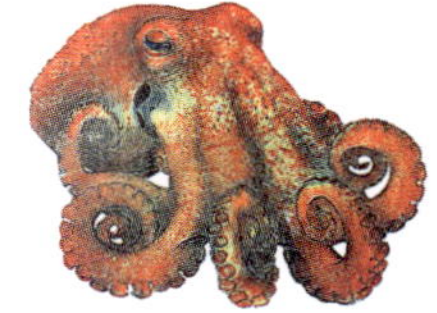

Thomas Shahan
www.thomasshahan.com
Thomas Shahan is an artist and photographer based out of Oklahoma, USA, who uses his background in printmaking to bring a creative approach to high-magnification macro photography. He has a BFA in Art from the University of Oklahoma and has worked as an imaging specialist for the Oregon Department of Agriculture, as a video-game artist and as a book illustrator. His photographs have appeared in *National Geographic*, on national television programmes and in museums throughout the world. Despite an interest in all fields of entomology, his passion lies with arachnids, specifically salticids.

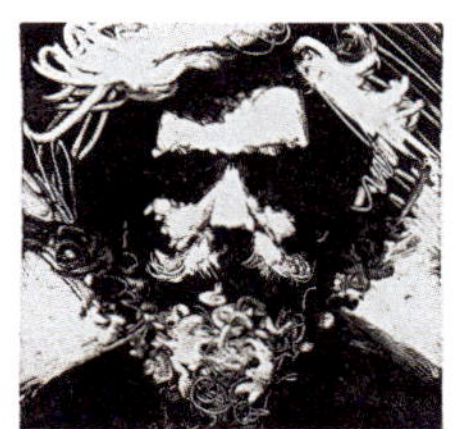

Tracy Simpson
www.tracy-simpson.com
Tracy Simpson is a self-taught printmaker who has honed the fine art of potato printing for 30 years. She returns over and over to themes of time, layers, loss, endurance, what we show others, what we keep to ourselves, what we show ourselves and what we keep from ourselves. Sometimes these themes show up as recognizable, if simply rendered, objects, and sometimes they are represented obliquely. It just depends.

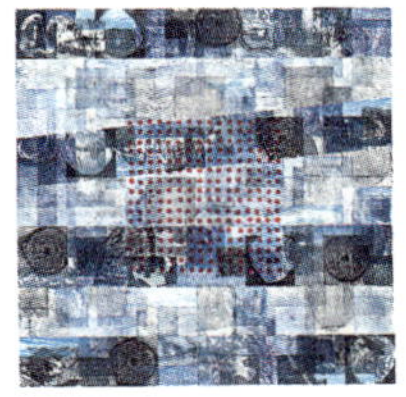

GLOSSARY

Aquatint: an etching method used to create a more subtle tonal range than could be achieved with line-etching techniques.

Baren: a hand tool used in a circular, burnishing motion to apply pressure to the back of the printing paper, thereby transferring the image from the printing plate.

Bleed: when the edge of the ink spreads into the weave of the paper. Can be caused by over-inking or printing paper that is too damp.

Brayer: a hard rubber roller used to evenly distribute ink.

Collagraph: can be made from almost any materials, collaged onto a stiff surface and printed either as a relief print or intaglio.

Colour separation: the process of isolating the individual colours that compose an artwork.

Cotton rag: also known as rag paper, or 'rag'. Made using cotton fibres or cotton from used cloth (rags) as the primary material. Cotton paper is stronger and more durable than wood pulp-based paper, and also absorbs ink more effectively.

Drypoint: a process in which marks are made on a smooth metal printing plate using a sharp, pointed instrument.

Edition: when a print is produced in multiples it is called an 'edition'. A limited edition means there is a specified number of prints produced of one image. An open edition means the artist will produce their print in any quantity they choose.

Emboss: to create a raised design on the surface of (usually damp) paper by applying pressure.

Etching: a design is scratched into a metal plate coated in acid-resistant ground. Acid is then used to bite the image into the metal plate.

Intaglio: uses incised (scratched) surfaces, such as drypoint, etching and some collagraphs.

Linocut: a linoleum printing block is easily carved using knives and gouges, then printed like a woodcut.

Lithography: the image is drawn on a smooth stone or plate using greasy crayons. The stone or plate is dampened and ink is applied with a roller. The greasy drawn image repels the water and holds the oily ink while the rest of the stone's surface does the opposite. The artwork is printed using a press.

Monoprint/monotype: no two prints are identical, though many of the same elements may be present. A monotype image is painted directly onto a smooth unaltered plate and then transferred to paper.

Photogravure: a photographic technique used with aquatint.

Planograph: printing from a flat surface, i.e. monoprints and screen prints.

Pochoir: a direct method for hand-colouring through a stencil.

Registration: The process of lining up colours with precision, when printing from multiple plates onto a single piece of paper

Relief: printing from raised surfaces, i.e. stamps, potato, wood and lino.

Risograph: a mechanical process using a printer that looks like a photocopier but works like a screen printer. It lays down a matrix of highly coloured ink dots onto the surface of the paper. The placement of the dots is dictated by the stencil that is created for each colour.

Screen print (serigraph, silkscreen): a mesh is stretched tightly over a frame. An image is cut from a stencil or exposed onto a photosensitive emulsion. The image areas are open mesh through which ink or paint is forced with a squeegee, while the negative space is blocked by the cured emulsion or stencil.

Tooth: refers to the roughness of the surface of paper - the more tooth, the more surface texture.

Woodcut: one of the oldest and simplest forms of printmaking. Tools can be used to cut the image into a block of wood. Paper is placed over the inked block and rubbed by hand or passed through a press to transfer the ink from block to paper to create the image.

INDEX

Page numbers in *italics* refer to illustrations

PICTURE CREDITS

pp. 4, 10-13, 42, 43, 76, 77, 83, 94, 95 © Eve Blackwood
p. 6 © Karen Wicks
p. 9 © Amanda Outcalt
p. 17 © The Saul Steinberg Foundation/Artists Rights Society (ARS), NY/DACS, London 2024
p. 18 © Koichi Yamamoto
p. 21 © Bryan Christopher Baker
pp. 22, 23 © Claire Drury
p. 24 © Kasey Golden
pp. 26-7 © Orpheas Tziagkidis and Raubdruckerin, Berlin 2017
p. 31 © Patricia Hardmeier
pp. 32, 33, 49-51 © Lily Vie
pp. 34-5 © Georgina Bown
p. 36 © Thomas Shahan
p. 39 © Tracy Simpson
pp. 40-1 © Jane Ormes
p. 45 © Laura Crehuet Berman
p. 46 © Clare Youngs
p. 55 © Rachel Newling
pp. 56, 57 © Paul Farrell
pp. 58, 59 © Asimina Hollingworth
p. 60 © LaToya Hobbs
pp. 62, 75 © Adam Larkum
p. 65 © Imi Maufe
pp. 66, 67 © Jennifer Zee
pp. 68-71 © Brenda Holtam
pp. 72, 73 © John Pedder
p. 79 © Marjorie Accarier
p. 80 © James and Malissa Brown
pp. 84, 85 © Howard Vie
p. 87 © Matthieu Roussel
pp. 90, 91 © Steph Renshaw
pp. 92, 93 © Emma Willemse
p. 97 © Anthony Connolly
pp. 100-1 © Ade Adesina
p. 103 © Sara Ogilvie
p. 104 © Jonny Hannah
p. 107 Illustrator and printmaker, PRINT IS NOT DEAD! by Natalia Ros & ceramist, Sanfangs/Sandra Rubio
p. 109 Courtesy artist Delita Martin and Galerie Myrtis Copyright: @Delita Martin
p. 110 © Monyee Chau

ACKNOWLEDGEMENTS

Thanks to Laura Paton for the light touch of her guiding hand, Susannah Jayes for working tirelessly to secure these artists' images and to Selwyn Leamy, a trusted and valued friend who not only set this process in motion but got me over the finish line.

This book is dedicated to Ian, Rowan and Gil, without whom all of this would be pointless, and to Derek Blackwood, my lovely dad, who shared his passion for all things creative with us from an early age and made making art an essential part of daily life. I am eternally grateful.

ABOUT THE AUTHOR

Eve Blackwood is a Scottish artist and educator who lives in London. She has worked as an illustrator, independent filmmaker, printmaker and BBC editor, and is currently an art teacher. She makes art every day and aims to inspire others to do the same.